RULES FOR REFS: SOCCER '01-02

By Carl P. Schwartz, Referee Contributor

Referee Enterprises, Inc., Franksville, Wis.

Rules for Refs: Soccer '01-02
by Carl P. Schwartz, Contributor, *Referee* **Magazine**

Copyright © 2001 by Referee Enterprises, Inc.
P.O. Box 161, Franksville, Wis. 53126.

Cover design by Lisa Martin

ISBN 1-58208-023-2

Printed in the United States of America.

Acknowledgment

This book is intended to supplement the rulebooks and casebooks published by the National Federation of State High School Associations (NFHS), the National Collegiate Athletic Association (NCAA) as well as the *Laws of the Game* as published by the United States Soccer Federation (USSF) and used throughout international soccer.

Referee wants to thank the NFHS, NCAA and USSF for their invaluable assistance providing interpretations, advice and guidance, which appear in this book.

Table of Contents

Introduction

There are some changes within each of the three major codes that govern soccer in this country, but there is good news. The changes that affect the play of the game are minor. Moreover, for the most part, the codes are getting closer to each other in their wording and interpretation. Most of the changes simply clarify language, add more caseplays that bring the rules to life and help referees officiate their contests. With up-to-date, technically accurate information, you stand a better chance of making better decisions during your contests.

This text hopes to educate. Certainly, rule changes and rule differences are important, but I have tried to show you there is more.

As the contributing editor of *Referee*'s soccer material, I often edit the work of other authors. But two topics really sparked my interest this year and I wanted a chance to share them. I've long admired FIFA President Joseph Blatter's writings in *FIFA News*. But this time, his message strikes a special note to referees — call the game as written in the *Laws of the Game* and the IFAB won't have to add new Laws. As an assessor, either sitting high in the stands or in the pressbox, I'm able to see patterns. Perhaps due to my experience, those patterns emerge clearly. When the referee also spots the trend and takes action, the game goes well. Either missing the patterns or taking inappropriate action causes referees to lose match control and suffer damage to their hard-earned reputations.

There are many others to thank: C. Cliff McCrath of the NCAA soccer rules committee, Alfred Kleinaitis, USSF manager of referee development and education and Tim Flannery of the NFHS. Dan Heldman contributed to the technical accuracy of the text as well as continues to be a good friend. His thoughtful comments over the past year have contributed much to *Referee* products. I thank them, as well as author David Keller, for their contributions. Keller is a bank CEO, able soccer administrator and a splendid referee. He was selected to work the 2001 AYSO World Games.

Good luck in your games ahead.

— *Carl P. Schwartz*

Chapter 1

2001-02 NFHS Rule Changes

By Carl P. Schwartz

The NFHS soccer rules committee made several changes this year. Most changes eliminate rules differences between NFHS and NCAA and FIFA/USSF. Make certain you enforce the correct rules for the contest that you are officiating.

The 10 committee members, meeting Jan. 7-8 in Indianapolis, plus representatives from the NISOA and USSF, discussed the changes and their rationale.

NFHS-registered referees should attend state association training and follow state interpretations or explanations.

Goalkeeper Time Limit (12-7-1)

Beginning with the 2001-02 season, goalkeepers in NFHS soccer no longer will be limited to four steps. Rather, they will have six seconds to release the ball into play after taking control of the ball with their hands within their own penalty area. During that interval, the keeper may hold the ball, bounce it or throw it into the air and catch it. Previously, goalkeepers were limited to four steps in any direction. With the new rule, there is no limit on the number of steps within the six-second period. That ruling is now consistent among all governing bodies.

"That change means that time wasting by goalkeepers with

the ball in their hands or arms is now measured in time rather than distance," said Tim Flannery, assistant director of the NFHS and editor of NFHS soccer publications. Delete 12-7-5

> **Play 1:** Keeper A1 catches the ball after a shot on goal. Well within the six-second time limit, A1 uses nine steps to run 15 yards with the ball and releases an overhand throw some 50 yards to A9.
>
> **Ruling 1:** Legal. Continue playing.

Upper levels of play have already given us examples of goalkeepers throwing the ball 60-65 yards to a teammate in an offside position. It's still offside. The exceptions to being penalized for an offside position include if the attacker receives the ball directly from a goalkick, corner kick or throw-in. In the play above, if A1 threw the ball directly to A9, standing in an offside position, who became involved in active play, A9 is penalized for offside. *Editor's note: Some state associations adopted this rule change for the 2000-01 season.*

Revised Definition of a Throw-in (15-1-2)

The soccer rules committee eliminated "equal force" from the throw-in definition, eliminating the requirement that referees judge whether both hands were used equally. The rule becomes: "The ball shall be thrown in any direction from the point where it crossed the touchline by a player who is facing the field of play and has both feet on the ground on or behind the touchline. The thrower shall use both hands and shall deliver the ball from behind and over the head in one continuous movement." That change is now consistent with FIFA. The NCAA still dictates the thrower "shall use both hands equally."

"This rule change brings back into focus the key elements of the throw-in," Flannery said. For years, referees have listened to fans complain that it had to be an illegal throw-in because, "Hey Ref, the ball is spinning." Spin is acceptable; a ball thrown in largely with one hand is not.

> **Play 2:** Team A is awarded a throw-in. Player A6, who has the use of only one arm, takes a throw-in that is legal in all other aspects. The referee allows that.
>
> **Ruling 2:** Correct procedure. So long as all the other elements are correctly applied, that throw-in gets the ball into play.

Subs on Throw-ins (3-3-4)

To make better use of the allowed playing time, the rules committee will allow unlimited substitutions by the team without the ball to enter the contest when the team with the ball chooses to substitute. However, substitutions on the opposing team must have reported to the scoring table before the stoppage of play occurs. The revised rule will read: "The team in possession of the ball from a throw-in may substitute. If the team in possession of the ball chooses to substitute, the opposing team may also substitute at that time." The change makes the NFHS ruling consistent with NCAA rules. The current 3-3-4 becomes 3-3-5. The current 3-3-5 becomes 3-3-6.

Flannery said that the defending team may not send a substitute to the scoring table after the dead ball occurs because the team in possession has a substitute ready to enter the game. Flannery added: "With substitutions freely allowed on a throw-in, the amount of playing time will be increased by permitting both teams to substitute at the same stoppage of play. That will improve the flow of the game by cutting down on the number of times substitutions are made."

Play 3: Team A is awarded a throw-in. A12, B14 and B16 had all reported to the scoring table before the ball went across the touchline. The referee allows A12 to replace A5, but does not allow B14 and B16 to enter.

Ruling 3: Incorrect decision. The rule change permits all three players to enter.

Play 4: Team A is awarded a throw-in. A12 reported to the scoring table before the ball went across the touchline. The coach of team B, trailing 2-1, sees that he can save a few seconds by substituting now, so he sends B13 to report and enter on that stoppage of play.

Ruling 4: The referee properly denies the substitution at that stoppage. Based on 3-4-1d, B13 must have reported to the table before the dead ball. Allow B13 to enter at the next team B substitution opportunity.

Players Entering When Team is Short-handed

Previously, it was not clear when a player could reenter the game in various situations when a team was playing short (3-3-2a, 3-3-2c, 3-4-1c). Examples are injuries, players with blood on their uniform or late-arriving players. Additional rules 3-3-7 and 3-3-8 address procedures for players entering the game after starting the contest short-handed. When a team elects or is required to play short-handed, for reasons other than misconduct, a player or players can reenter the game during a *stoppage of play*. Previously the wording was "the next legal substitution opportunity." Remember that a team must have at least seven players for the contest to start (3-1-2).

Play 5: A9 and B1 are contesting for a loose ball when B1 goes down with a severe injury. No penalty is involved, but the game is temporarily suspended due to the injury. When play is ready to resume, the referee: a) awards a throw-in to team B because B3 had control of the ball before it became loose and was contested by A9 and B1; b) administers a dropped ball because no team had clear possession at the time the game was temporarily suspended.

Ruling 5: The referee was incorrect in a), but correctly followed the ruling in b). If B3 had clear possession moments *after* A9 and B1 contested for the ball (i.e., it took the referee a few seconds to evaluate the injury and decide on a stoppage), then award team B an indirect free kick. (9-2-1)

Shoes (4-1-1c)

The change simplifies the rule by eliminating specifications and taking into consideration new technology in shoe design and construction. "New technology makes it difficult to determine whether shoes are safe based on depth and width," Flannery said. "Many shoes manufactured today are considered safe but do not meet the specifications of the previous rule. The committee is more concerned with the safety of the athlete and believes that the old rule made it difficult for coaches and officials to adequately inspect shoes."

"Shoes must be worn by all participants in a game. Shoes with soles containing metal (aluminum, magnesium, titanium, etc.) leather, rubber, nylon or plastic cleats, studs or bars, whether molded as part of the sole or detachable, are allowed as long as the referee does not consider them dangerous. Shoes shall not be altered in any way that makes them unsafe."

Knee Braces (4-2-1g)

The committee also revised language regarding knee braces. The last sentence was deleted and replaced with language stating that "any covering (sleeve) recommended by the manufacturer may be worn."

"Technology has enabled manufacturers to design braces specifically for athletes," Flannery said. "The soccer rules committee is concerned about the safety of the player first and foremost and recognizes that altering the brace may void its effectiveness." The rule may compromise a manufacturer's warranty.

Officials' Uniforms (5-1-3a)

A change gives state high school associations authority to determine the color of shirts for officials. "The committee wants to clarify that each state association should determine the color of officials' shirts in its state," Flannery said. "The old language appeared more like a mandate than a guideline. The committee strongly suggests that only NFOA or association logos be allowed on officials' shirts." White caps are no longer listed as an alternative.

Point of Emphasis

Each year, the NFHS committee chooses a number of items for special focus. Referees, coaches and players should heed these points prior to and during games.

Player safety: Safety is the number one priority in any game. When a player is injured or presumed to be injured the game should be stopped. If it is determined that the players were faking the injuries, they should be cautioned for unsportsmanlike behavior. (12-8-1)

Play 6: As team A quickly attacks the team B goal with four attackers against two defenders, B7 falls to the ground in the center circle. When parents and coaches scream that B7 is injured, the referee sees the prone B7 and stops play. As soon as the referee whistles play dead, B7 gets up and says that he is fine and can continue in the game.

Ruling 6: Caution and display a yellow card to B7, inform the scorer and both coaches of the reason for the caution, allow team B to substitute B12 for B7 and restart play with an indirect free kick at the location where B7 was when play was stopped.

Portable goals: In the interest of safety, portable goals shall be anchored, secured or counterweighted. Many injuries occur because goals are not properly stored or secured when not in use. Soccer goals are an attractive nuisance and those who are responsible for the storage or security of portable goals should go to extreme measures to discourage and prevent individuals from using them before or after practices or games.

Play 7: The home team is using portable goals. During the pregame inspection, the referee notices they are not anchored or secured in any way. The referee asks the home coach or host administrator to solve the problem. Two minutes before kickoff, the referee again checks the goals and finds them unsecured. The coach says he has no way of securing the goals. The referee refuses to start the game.

Ruling 7: Correct decision. Do not start a game with that unsafe condition. If necessary, wait a reasonable time for the home team to fix the problem. If they refuse, or cannot correct the problem in a reasonable time, leave the playing site and report the incident to the proper authority.

Sportsmanship: At the pregame conference, the head referee shall address coaches and players concerning aspects of good sportsmanship including excessive celebration, profanity and taunting. A short but firm statement by the official outlining the action that will be taken for unsporting behavior would be appropriate. It would be helpful to use specific examples of behavior that will not be tolerated to make the point. The officials need to enforce what has been communicated to the athletes and coaches in the pregame conference.

Ballholders: Home schools shall provide at least two ballholders. The soccer rules committee continues to encourage schools to make arrangements in advance to comply with this requirement. Every attempt should be made to secure two ball holders prior to starting a game. That should be addressed in coach's and official's pregame checklist. If ballholders are not provided, the referee shall report the situation to the proper authorities and start the game.

Shinguards: There continues to be concern with players modifying shinguards, thus jeopardizing their own safety. Shinguards shall not be altered, be worn properly and should afford each player's shins reasonable protection. The official should examine both shinguards to verify that they provide adequate protection to the shin of the player. Some state associations have dictated a specific number of inches between the shinguard and the ankle or the shinguard and the knee.

Caution/disqualification procedure: Whenever an official issues a yellow or red card, both coaches and the player shall be notified of the reason for the caution or disqualification. Officials can enlist one assistant referee to assist in the notification procedure. State associations may consider using a reporting area, designated prior to the game, where officials can notify scorer(s) and coaches the reason for cautions or disqualifications. The reporting area must be in an area that both scorers and coaches can hear and see the official. Some state associations have devised a written form that the referee must complete at the game's end. A copy goes to each team.

Soccer continues to be the fastest-growing sport overall in NFHS. In terms of participants, soccer ranks number five in popularity with just over 600,000 participants.

Chapter 2

2001 NCAA Rule Changes

By Carl P. Schwartz

Very few changes affect the play of the game. Most NCAA changes this year reflect more precise language to clear up any confusion, especially among those who deal with several rulemaking bodies. There are a large number of points of emphasis. Read and heed.

All the following changes were approved by committee vote at the February 2001 meeting of the NCAA Men's and Women's Soccer Rules Committee in Key Largo, Fla.

Referee once again thanks C. Cliff McCrath, NCAA soccer committee secretary-rules editor, for reviewing this text and for his ceaseless efforts to improve the game. Much of the background material to support this chapter was contained in the *NCAA News*.

Field Dimensions and Notification (1-1b)

The rule change inserts a sentence into the end of second paragraph: "Further, it is the responsibility of the home team to notify the visiting team — before the date of the game — of any changes in field dimensions, playing surface (e.g., from grass to artificial or vice versa) or location of the playing site."

The committee put some teeth into the new wording with a revised approved ruling. The new AR 1 reads: "If the field was constructed after 1995 and prior written mutual consent of the competing coaches has not been established, the game shall not begin and the referee shall file a report with the governing sports authority (see page 8)."

Play 1: As the referee, you show up at the gamesite one hour prior to the scheduled starting time. The visiting coach, excited at unexpectedly finding an artificial surface, angrily confronts you. After calming him down, you call the visiting athletic director to confirm no written notification was received. You call the host athletic director to see if written documentation of the changed surface can be produced. When no letter is produced by scheduled game start time, you tell the home coach there will be no contest. The home coach verbally curses you several times as you walk to your car and threatens you with a lawsuit.

Ruling 1: In addition to filing a report with the governing sports authority about the lack of written notification and not playing the game, include the coach's comments verbatim (including the vulgar language directed toward you). File a copy of the report with your assignor and NISOA chapter.

Goals (1-9) **and Goal Nets** (1-10)

"No other markings other than a single manufacturer's identification/logo *of appropriate size* may appear on the goalposts or the crossbar [or net] " The committee rewrote AR 5 to specify prohibited markings on the nets: "May goal nets be multicolored, lettered or reflect school names, logos, slogans or any other commercial design? **Ruling:** No."

Game Roster (3-2)

Delete from AR 22: " *… and if the score clearly reflects a winner, …*" The AR discussed overtime contests and a determination that a player not listed on the game roster scored a goal.

> **Play 2:** In the 78th minute, A20 scored team A's only goal in a 1-1 tie. During the overtime period, the team B sports information director asked for A20's name for the press release. It was not listed on the game roster.
>
> **Ruling 2:** Once the fourth official or assistant referee gets the referee's attention to suspend the game at a stoppage, the referee verifies that A20 was not listed on the official game roster. Using AR 22, the referee removes A20 from the game, nullifies the goal, ends the game and declares team B the victor.

Should that undesirable outcome occur in a contest you are working, expect to hear some harsh words spoken by frustrated people — coaches, players and fans. Before announcing the outcome, you might wish to have an institution representative (athletic director, campus security, etc.) nearby. Explain to them that you are about to announce something very controversial, tell them to expect some upset people and decide on a course of action. Then announce the decision and follow the plan you formulated.

Sample Timing Sheets (3-2d)

Delete both references to *"Teams shake hands"* at the 3:00 mark. Also change: "Introduce ball *shaggers*" to "Introduce ball *persons*."

Substitutes (3-4b)

Many people associated with the college game, including referees, were confused about how many substitutes the other team may substitute at a throw-in. Insert: "… also may substitute *up to 11 players* at that time."

> **Play 3:** A12, A13, B13, B14, B15 and B16 are all waiting at the scorer's table when the ball goes out for a team A throw-in. The referee allows A12 and A13 to enter, and then tells the team B coach that only two substitutes may enter at that time because that's all that team A substituted.
>
> **Ruling 3:** Incorrect ruling by the referee. When at least one team A player is at the table before the ball goes out of play, that team A player and all team B players already at the table may enter.

Delaying Tactics at Substitutions (3-4b)

Delete AR 26. Referees no longer need to stop the clock if they believe that the substitution procedure is being used to gain an unfair advantage. The clock automatically stops at each substitution (2000 change to 3-6).

Substitution Reentry Conditions (3-5b 2)

"Players *instructed* to leave the field of play because of a bleeding injury or blood…" Instructed replaces the word "required."

Substitution Restrictions, Exceptions (3-5b)

AR 33 now reads: "A player receives a caution but is not *replaced* at the time …" AR 34 now reads: "A player is cautioned and *replaced* at the time …" For both approved rulings, the former language was "removed from the game." Change AR 36 to read: "A player *instructed* to leave the field due to a bleeding injury or blood ..."

Reporting Into the Game (3-6)

Change the last sentence of the first paragraph to read: "In addition, the referee shall signal that the clock be stopped and beckon the substitute(s) onto the field." The wording makes the referee a more active agent in controlling substitutions. Now, the rule specifically states the referee is to signal to stop the clock. Also, the referee is specifically responsible for beckoning the substitutes onto the field. Insert new AR before AR 37: "Shall the referee also beckon a substitute(s) onto the field after the clock has been stopped? **Ruling:** Yes."

Change AR 42 to read: "When does a substitute become *a* field player of record?" Formerly, the wording was "become the field player of record." AR 42 Ruling now reads: "At the moment the referee signals the clock to be stopped." Formerly, a substitute became a field player of record when the referee beckoned or otherwise indicated that permission was given for the substitute to enter the field. Literally 99 percent of the time, you won't have a problem with a now-already-substituted-out player still on the field starting misconduct with an opponent. Should A12 replace A6, and A6, while still on the field, spit at B4, you would red card A6. If B4 retaliates by punching A6, you would also red card B4. Your dilemma — do you play 10 versus 10 or 10 versus 11? Remember that A12 is now the player of record and A6 was an outside agent still on the field after being substituted out. The game is restarted with team A up a player (11 to team B's 10). *Explanation:* Rule 5-4b AR 57 provides the answer. The issue pertains to the "active" player at the time of the incident. B4 had not been replaced (substituted for); A6 had. It was team B's misfortune, but the fact remains that A6 no longer was the player of record. The play would be no different than a player on the bench being ejected without the team playing short.

There are two new ARs to insert following AR 42: "Does a player(s) have to enter the field of play after the referee has signaled the clock to be stopped for a substitution(s)? **Ruling:** No. However, the player(s) shall be charged with one substitution entry." The second AR reads: "Multiple players have reported to the scorekeeper — or assistant referee — to enter the game as substitutes. The referee signals to stop the clock and the coach decides to hold one player back. Is that player charged with a substitution entry? **Ruling:** Yes."

That is a significant change. Formerly, when a substitute reported to the table and a substitution opportunity arose, the substitute was required to enter. Now the coach has some latitude, but at the cost of a charged substitution.

Changing Goalkeepers (3-7)

"The referee shall be notified when *a goalkeeping change* is made." Formerly the wording was when "any substitution for the goalkeeper." Insert a new AR following AR 44: "May a teammate on the field of play change positions with the goalkeeper? **Ruling:** Yes, provided it occurs during stoppage of play and all other rules pertaining to players' uniforms are satisfied (see Rule 4-2, 3)."

Do not allow teams to use switching onfield keepers as a delaying tactic in the closing moments of a tight game. If need be, you have the authority to stop the clock (6-3b 1). The prohibition regarding substituting a bench player for the goalkeeper before a penalty kick remains.

Player's Equipment (4-1b)

"Players shall wear shinguards under the stockings in the manner intended. The shinguards shall be professionally manufactured, age appropriate and not altered to decrease protection." Formerly shinguards had to "afford a reasonable degree of protection."

AR 46 says that no player may be exempted from wearing shinguards, even if wearing a knee brace.

Play 4: Player A14 will not wear shinguards, saying his coach doesn't make him wear them during practice. A16 is wearing shinguards appropriate for a U-8 player. A18 is wearing shinguards that have obviously been cut from eight inches down to three inches.

Ruling 4: A14, A16 and A18 may not participate until they are wearing legal shinguards that meet the requirements of 4-1b. Should one of them substitute into the game without wearing legal shinguards, follow 3-4g and allow a substitute (AR 27). The player entered the game with illegal equipment. If you had pointed out the improper equipment prior to the match and A14, A16 or A18 still entered the game without correcting the problem, they should be cautioned (4-5 Penalty, 12-14e). If A14, A16 or A18 is substituted out to correct the equipment, they are subject to the reentry conditions in 3-5.

Contrasting Colors (4-2)

The rule now reads: "Goalkeepers shall wear jerseys that distinguish them from all *field* players and referees." The new wording allows the home goalkeeper to wear a jersey color that matches the visiting goalkeeper.

Dangerous Articles (4-5)

Change first sentence of Penalty to read: "If the referee considers any article liable to cause injury, ... the referee shall signal the clock to be stopped and instruct the player to leave the field of play and remove the illegal article." The new interpretation directs the referee to stop the clock. Deny entry or reentry into the game as long as they are wearing the items you consider dangerous. Change the third sentence of Penalty to read: "After being instructed to leave the field, a player shall not *reenter* the game ..."

Change AR 50 Ruling to read: "The referee shall *instruct the player to leave* the field until he or she conforms with Rule 4-5, 6." Formerly the wording was "The player shall be sent off" which might have led to confusion with an ejection (red card) for those referees who work under several codes. Change AR 52 to read: "If a player was *instructed to leave* the field ..." for the same reason.

Jewelry (4-6)

"A player shall not wear any jewelry including earrings, chains, charms, watches, hair clips, *tongue studs or items associated with piercing — visible or not visible.*" Change the first sentence of AR 55: "... required to wear *items* (crosses, rosary beads, yarmulkes, etc.) not conforming to ..." The additional forbidden items relate to changing societal norms. The more generic term item replaces the words "garments, jewelry." That does not mean referees all have to become experts in religious matters. None of the items are "required" by the religion with which they are commonly associated. They are "permitted" and, indeed, even encouraged. The fact that an item is religious in nature does *not* mean that it is mandated.

> **Play 5:** During the pregame walk around, you notice A9 talking to A6, and see a flash of metal in A6's mouth. You ask A6 to take the piercing out and he says that what you saw was orthodontic metalwork and he doesn't have any piercing, but he refuses to have his mouth inspected. Going to the team A coach, you tell the coach that A6 may not participate while wearing the jewelry.
>
> **Ruling 5:** Correct procedure. Do not argue with A6. If he protests or offers an explanation, do not get in a confrontation with the player. Speak to the coach or authority figure. Do not allow A6 to participate with jewelry.

Referee's Uniform (5-2)

"All referees shall dress in the prescribed uniform and wear shoes that are *predominantly* black. Shirts of the same color and style shall be alike for all officials and shall be in contrast to those worn by the competing teams. It is permissible ..." The old text dictated the black referee jersey with alternate colors possible. Your NISOA chapter or conference will let you know the primary color of choice. The rule also changed the shoe color from "primarily black" to predominantly black.

Discretionary Power (5-5e 1)

"If the (injured) player is not the goalkeeper, *and medical personnel are beckoned to attend the player(s),* the referee shall instruct the players to leave ..."

Insert two new ARs to follow 5-5e: "The referee signals the clock be stopped to assess a player's injuries and it is determined that medical personnel are not needed. Does the player have to leave the field of play? **Ruling:** No." The second AR is: "Multiple players appear to be injured in a single incident and medical personnel are beckoned onto the field of play. Do all players involved in the injury situation have to leave the field of play? **Ruling:** Yes, unless one of the players is the goalkeeper. The goalkeeper is allowed to remain."

Insert new AR to follow AR 71: "When may a referee reverse a decision involving a sudden-victory goal? **Ruling:** Any time prior to signing the official NCAA box score form or leaving the site of competition (see Rules 5-3-a and 6-4)." Proper mechanics during such a controversial incident would be to immediately look at both assistants (and the fourth official) as soon as the goal is scored — before awarding and signaling the goal. Too often, referees simply look at the lead assistant and signal the goal. Get all the information from your partners first!

Timekeeper (6-3b 7)

The timekeeper shall stop the clock "When a player is *instructed to leave the field* for an equipment change." Delete subparagraph (6), which directed the timekeeper to stop the clock for a substitution. The rules now direct the referee to signal that the clock be stopped (see 3-6 above).

End of Game (7-3)

Insert a new paragraph: "Section 3. The end of the game shall occur after time has expired and the referee has signed the official NCAA box score form or left the site of the competition (see Rules 5-3a and 6-4)." The end of the game had not been specifically defined. The referee's jurisdiction continues in effect until the end of the game.

> **Play 6:** The score is tied in the 88th minute when A6 scores a goal. A6 was level with the second-to-last defender, so to B3 it was a controversial offside decision. After the final horn, as you are walking toward the locker room where you agreed to meet the official scorer to sign the box score form, B3 steps in front of you and utters an offensive tirade. As the three referees are passing through the gate, B3 bumps the assistant that made the controversial decision.
>
> **Ruling 6:** The referee still has jurisdiction over the contest. Once in the locker room, ask the team B coach to join you in the locker room, explain what B3 did to deserve the ejection, and without displaying a card, tell the team B coach that you will report the ejection. Record B3's ejection on the box score form, sign it and make your game report to the governing sports authority. Send a copy to your assignor and NISOA chapter.

Method of Scoring (10-1)

Change third paragraph to read: "If *a* defending player deliberately *handles* the ball in an attempt to prevent a goal, it shall be scored a goal if it goes in." The changes add more precise language in describing the foul.

Suspended Games (10-9)

If the conditions leading to a suspended game persist and the game "is not resumed *the same day*, the game shall be considered 'no contest' if it hasn't progressed to 70 minutes."

Ejections (12-15g)

Referees shall eject a player, coach or team representative who "uses offensive, insulting or abusive language *or gestures.*"

Points of Emphasis

- Hash Mark (1-2)
- Sample Timing Sheet (3-2d)
- Clock Stops on Substitution (3-6)
- Substitution Entry (3-6)
- Shinguard Requirements (4-1b)
- Jewelry (4-6)
- Substitution for Injury (5-5e)
- Official Time Kept by Scoreboard Only (6-3f)
- End of Game (7-3)
- "No Contest" Redefined (10-9)
- Shirt-Pulling Prohibited (12-4)
- Language Abuse, Zero Tolerance (12-14d, 12-15g)
- One Yellow Maximum Per Game (12-14)
- Card Accumulation Chart (12-18)

Chapter 3

Laws of the Game Changes

By Carl P. Schwartz

The 115th annual meeting of the International Football Association Board (IFAB) was held in Edinburgh, Scotland, on March 10, 2001. The amendments to the *Laws of the Game* and various instructions and directives are below.

Referee is grateful to U.S. Soccer Manager of Referee Development and Education Alfred Kleinaitis for reviewing the text (based on IFAB circular 750 and USSF's 2001 Memorandum). Caseplays and rulings are provided by *Referee* and do not represent official guidance from USSF. Some rulings are oriented toward general recreational soccer where the strict application of the *Laws of the Game* is not the same as in an upper-division or professional match. The Law changes go into effect July 1, or as directed by your state referee administrator.

1. Notes on the *Laws of the Game*

"Subject to the agreement of the national associations ... the Laws may be modified in their application for players under 16 years of age, for women players, for veteran players (older than 35) *and for players with disabilities.*"

USSF Advice to Referees: Law changes to accommodate disabilities under the provision are intended for special competitions sanctioned by and under the authority of USSF, which is responsible for reviewing and approving such modifications.

2. The Number of Players (3)

Under Decisions of the International Board, Decision 2: *"A team official* may convey tactical instructions to the players during the match and must return to his position after doing so. All team officials must remain within the confines of the technical area, where such an area is provided, and they must behave in a responsible manner."

Reason: The new text recognizes that tactical instructions may be given by different team officials during the match provided the person returns to his or her position after giving those instructions and behaves in a responsible manner. The statement that the team official must return *immediately* to his or her position has been removed.

USSF Advice to Referees: Under most circumstances, the referee (assisted by the assistant referee and/or the fourth official) should ensure that no more than one team official is giving tactical instructions at any one time. Referees are reminded that the requirement to return to their position does not mean that the team official must be seated.

Play 1: The team A coach moves to the front corner of the technical area. While there, he (a) shouts tactical instructions to his players and returns to the bench, (b) twice steps forward of the boundary line, interfering with the assistant referee, (c) continuously shouts dissenting remarks at every decision made by the referee that goes against his team or (d) remains there for five minutes after giving instructions.

Ruling 1: In (a), take no action. In (b), a fourth official or assistant must use personality and persuasion to convince the coach to remain behind the technical area line, for everyone's safety. If those warnings go unheeded, call the referee over to deal with the matter. In (c), the referee might wait for a stoppage in play, ask that the restart be delayed momentarily, move to the coach and inform him that his irresponsible behavior will be reported (the same as a yellow card, but no card is displayed, *Advice to Referees* 5.10). In (d), handle the situation as in case (b) and ask the coach to return to his position at the team bench.

3. Fouls and Misconduct (12)

Under Indirect Free Kick, delete bullet point five:

• Wastes time

Also, under Decisions of the International Board, Decision 3, delete the final paragraph:

• The goalkeeper is considered to be guilty of time wasting if he holds the ball in his hands or arms for more than five to six seconds.

Reason: Both texts are no longer necessary because of the alteration to Law 12 in 2000, which stated that a goalkeeper is permitted to control the ball with his hands or arms for up to six seconds.

USSF Advice to Referees: That is an editorial change to make the Law more internally consistent and does not affect the application of Law 12. Referees should review Memorandum 2000 regarding the procedures for enforcing the six-second time limit.

4. Fouls and Misconduct (12)

Under Disciplinary Sanctions, add new text: Only a player *or substitute or substituted player* may be shown the red or yellow card.

Reason: That clarifies the use of the red and yellow cards.

USSF Advice to Referees: That addition to Law 12 enforces prior guidance regarding who may commit misconduct and therefore be shown a card. Referees are reminded that it is improper to show cards to anyone other than players, substitutes or substituted players. If irresponsible behavior is committed by anyone else in the immediate area of the field, the circumstances must be included in the game report. "Substituted players" refers to any player who has been substituted and, although not permitted to return to the field, remains in his team's area.

Play 2: The coach, standing within the technical area, shouts dissenting comments to the referee. The referee jogs to within 20 yards of the touchline and displays the yellow card to the coach.

Ruling 2: Incorrect action. The referee may not display misconduct cards to coaches, assistant coaches, team doctors or other non-players within the technical area. One possible mechanic is for the referee to say to the coach, "Coach, your irresponsible behavior will be noted on my game report." That is the equivalent to a yellow card for a coach. Should you need to send off a coach, do not display a red card; rather say, "Coach, you are dismissed." Turn, move well away (center circle or far-side assistant) and wait an appropriate period for the coach to collect his belongings and depart sight and sound from the field.

5. Fouls and Misconduct (12)

Under Sending-Off Offenses, add after No. 7: A player who has been sent off must leave the vicinity of the field of play and the technical area.

Reason: That clarifies the situation for players who have been sent off.

USSF Advice to Referees: In many circumstances, particularly involving youth players, it may not be possible to apply that requirement strictly. The primary objective of the requirement is to ensure that a player who has been sent off will no longer in any way interfere with, participate in or otherwise be involved in subsequent play. The failure of a player who has been sent off to meet that objective cannot result in any further disciplinary action against the player by the referee, but all details of any incident must be included in the game report.

Play 3: Adult player, A9, was sent off after 65 minutes of play. A9 leaves the field and sits on the team bench. The referee restarts the game and continues play.

Ruling 3: Incorrect action. With an adult player, typically you wait until the player is "sight and sound" away from the playing field before restarting the game. Allow A9 a minute or two to gather sweats and other personal belongings. If A9 is still at the bench area after about 90 seconds, look to the team coach to encourage A9 to depart.

Play 4: A8, a U-14 player, is sent off for violent conduct after 50 minutes. The team A coach calls A8 to sit on the bench next to him.

Ruling 4: Given risk management for youth sports, that is an appropriate action. As the referee, you do not want to

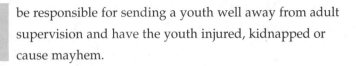

be responsible for sending a youth well away from adult supervision and have the youth injured, kidnapped or cause mayhem.

6. Fouls and Misconduct (12)

Under Decisions of the International Board, delete Decision 1.

Reason: That confirms the sanction to be taken, as stated in the *Questions and Answers on the Laws of the Game*, when an object is thrown at an opponent from a distance.

USSF Advice to Referees: Referees should review the recent memorandum on "placing restarts" for additional details regarding the above reference to Questions and Answers. In brief, the location for any foul or misconduct involving a thrown object is not where the action begins but where the object strikes or would have struck, if that location is on the field of play.

7. Procedures to Determine the Winner of a Match

"The Golden Goal and taking kicks from the penalty mark are methods of determining the winning team where competition rules require there to be a winning team after a match has been drawn."

Golden Goal procedures:

• During the period of extra time played at the end of normal playing time, the team which scores the first goal is declared the winner.

• If no goals are scored the match is decided by kicks from the penalty mark.

The text under Kicks from the Penalty Mark remains unchanged.

Reason: To formally recognize the approval by the IFAB of the

Golden Goal as one of the possible procedures to determine a winner.

USSF Advice to Referees: Referees must be aware of any league, tournament or competition rules that define when and how a match that is tied at the end of regulation time must be continued until there is a winner. The Law change recognizes the option of the Golden Goal (also called sudden death) as one means of accomplishing that objective.

Play 5: A new U-12 coach heard about the Law changes. The game ends as a 2-2 draw. The adult coach directs the youth referee to continue to play until a Golden Goal is scored for (a) regular season league play or (b) tournament preliminary round games.

Ruling 5: In both cases, the tied game ends as a tie, unless specific league or tournament rules direct otherwise. (It would be very rare!) Further, the youth referee should report the actions of the coach.

Instructions and Directives

In addition to the Law changes, the IFAB introduced specific instructions and directives that go into effect immediately. They include the following:

Holding and pulling. The IFAB expressed its concern at the amount of holding and pulling that was prevalent in soccer today. It recognized that not every instance of holding and pulling of jerseys and shorts was unsporting behavior, as is also the case with a deliberate handball. It expressed regret, however, that referees were not applying the Laws fully in dealing with blatant cases of holding and pulling and issued the following mandatory instruction:

Referees are instructed that, in the case of blatant holding and pulling, the offense must be sanctioned by a direct free kick, or a penalty kick if the offense is committed inside the penalty area, and the player must be cautioned for unsporting behavior.

USSF Advice to Referees: Holding or pulling the jersey of an opponent has always been a penal foul, subject to the decision of the referee that the action was not trifling. The above mandatory instruction serves to emphasize to referees that their standards for making such decisions must take into account the blatant and cynical nature of the action, regardless of its effect.

Treatment of injured players. The IFAB considered the problems caused by injuries to players. It was of the opinion that referees should allow players to return to the field of play as soon as possible after they have recovered from injury. In that respect, and in the case of players returning from treatment for a bleeding injury, referees may be assisted by the fourth official, when one has been appointed to the match.

The IFAB also expressed its concern at the loss of playing time caused by the assessment of injuries and their removal from the field of play. The safety of the players must always be the main priority, however referees are instructed to add the full amount of time lost for those and any other reasons at the end of each period of play.

USSF Advice to Referees: The practical effects of that instruction are:

• To add the option (as decided by the referee and discussed in the pregame conference) to involve the fourth official in confirming that any bleeding or blood-soaked uniform problem has been corrected.

• To allow a player who is off the field, with the permission of the referee, for treatment of an injury or for correction of a bleeding or blood-soaked uniform problem to return to the field, with the permission of the referee, while play is continuing.

• To require referees to add the full measure of time lost due to injury.

Keeping in mind the ultimate purpose of the instruction (ensuring that the full strengths of both teams are participating in play), USSF advises referees that, if a fourth official has not been appointed to a match, the referee may authorize the assistant referees to inspect players for the correction of bleeding or blood-soaked uniform problems.

Experiments to the *Laws of the Game*. The experiment involving the "two-referee" system of control (two referees with whistles paired with two assistant referees) has ended and will not be adopted.

The "10-yard advancement" experiment will be continued for another year, with the additional requirement that advancement will cease at the penalty-area line.

Advertising. The IFAB noted with concern that its decision taken on March 4, 1995 prohibiting advertising and club logos on goal nets and corner flags, was not being respected. Such advertising *is not permitted* in the *Laws of the Game* and FIFA was asked to take action against clubs that do not respect those instructions.

Celebration of a goal. The IFAB recognized that the celebration of a goal is an important and emotional part of soccer and relaxed the earlier statement in FIFA Circular 579 of Jan. 23, 1996, that players removing their jersey when celebrating a goal should be cautioned. Players will no longer be cautioned if they remove their shirt but they will be cautioned for unsporting behavior if their celebrations are provocative and intended to incite or ridicule opponents or opposing spectators. Players guilty of excessive time wasting while celebrating a goal will also be cautioned.

USSF Advice to Referees: The purpose of this guidance is to remove the requirement that a player who removes his shirt while celebrating a goal is to be cautioned automatically. The IFAB has emphasized the continued importance of dealing with celebrations that incite, are provocative or take an excessive amount of time.

Players wearing eyeglasses. Sympathy was expressed for players, especially young players, who need to wear eyeglasses. It was accepted that new technology has made sports eyeglasses much safer, both for the players who wear them and for other players.

While the referee has the final decision on the safety of players' equipment, the IFAB expects that they will take full account of modern technology and the improved safety features of eyeglass design when making their decision.

USSF Advice to Referees: Referees must not interpret the above statement to mean either that "sports glasses" must automatically be considered safe or that glasses that are not manufactured to be worn during sports are automatically to be considered unsafe. The referee must make the final decision: the IFAB has simply recognized that new technology has made safer the wearing of glasses during play.

Artificial surfaces. The IFAB took note of major developments in artificial playing surfaces and FIFA's quality standards in that regard. Artificial surfaces are already permitted in 2002 World Cup qualifying matches.

Chapter 4

A Look Back

By Carl P. Schwartz

NFHS
Rules Interpretations

Any person having questions about the interpretation of NFHS rules should contact the rules interpreter designated by his or her state high school association.

Throw-in Awarded to Opponents (15-1-5)

"If the ball fails to enter the field of play on a throw-in, the ball is awarded to the opponent at the spot of the infraction."
Rationale: Players must execute the throw-in properly or an opponent will obtain possession of the ball. In past years, improper throw-ins delayed the game and were permitted to be retaken.

This change creates a rule difference. Be certain that everyone who works several codes of rules understands that this change applies only to NFHS contests. Equally important, be sure that everyone understands when a throw-in is legally in play. Once any portion of the ball, whether in the air or on the ground, breaks the plane of the outer edge of the touchline, the ball is in play. *Editor's note: The 2001 version of* Advice to Referees *will specify that the ball must also leave the thrower's hand. That common sense addition should apply to your rulings.*

> **Play 1**: A9 takes a throw-in while facing at a 45-degree angle to the touchline. A9 throws the ball 20 yards, but at no time was any portion of the ball over any portion of the touchline.
>
> **Ruling 1**: Award a throw-in to team B from where A9 took the throw-in.

> **Play 2:** Same as play 1, except A9's throw breaks the plane of the boundary line before curving back out of play, completely across the touchline.
>
> **Ruling 2:** Since the ball legally entered play for a moment before crossing wholly over the boundary line, award a throw-in to team B from the location where the ball left play. That ruling is no different than in past years.

Excessive Celebration Added to List of "Soft Reds"

(12-8-2b, 18-1-1p).

The definition of excessive celebration is added: "Any delayed, excessive or prolonged act by which players attempt to focus attention upon themselves or prohibit a timely restart of the game, has players leaving the field, removing a jersey or is not team oriented." *Rationale:* The ruling defines excessive celebration, which is penalized with a yellow and red card (disqualification). The team may substitute for the disqualified player under those circumstances. Some referees know that as a "soft red" card. Referees must disqualify players or coaches for excessive celebrations after the scoring of a goal.

Play 3: With the score standing at 4-0, reserve player A22 scores. A22 (a) runs about 15 yards, skips a few steps and jumps into a teammate's arms or (b) runs to the corner flag, removes the post from the ground and swings it over his head several times.

Ruling 3: Referees must differentiate between normal excitement and excessive celebration. A22 should be joyful, run, yell and seek approval from his teammates. In (a), the referee should allow a few seconds of enthusiastic cheering, then jog toward the jubilant players and remind them that it is time to position themselves for the ensuing kickoff. In (b), as soon as A22 removes the corner flag from the ground, the referee should withdraw his red and yellow cards, display them directly over his own head, inform A22 of his disqualification and inform both coaches. Allow team A to substitute for A22 before letting team B kick off.

Play 4: In the last seconds of a preseason tournament championship match, A5 scores a goal which puts team A ahead, 4-3. The team A coach is overjoyed, jumps up and down with enthusiasm and in (a), takes two steps onto the field as he is jumping, or (b), runs into the penalty area to hug A5 and lifts the player from the ground repeatedly over the next 15 seconds.

Ruling 4: In (a), the referee should remind the coach to stay behind the boundary lines surrounding the team and coaching area. In (b), the referee must disqualify the team A coach. Display the red and yellow card together. Allow the coach a moment to gather his belongings and depart the playing area. Report the incident to the state association.

Solid Colored Socks 4-1-1(a)

"Both stockings shall be the same single dominant color but not necessarily the color of the jersey." *Rationale:* The change was announced in last year's rulebook to become effective for the 2000-01 season. The rule outlaws "bumble-bee," tie-dyed, polka-dot and paisley socks. Play the game and report any infractions.

Play 5: The coach of team A tells the referee that he has written authorization from his athletic director to wear last year's tie-dyed socks. Further, the coach produces the letter, which states that funds are budgeted in next year's budget to purchase socks.

Ruling 5: That written authorization is not valid. Team A may not wear tie-dyed socks during a contest. Should team A have no other socks available, play the game. The referee shall file a written report with the state association within 24 hours.

Points of Emphasis

1. Uniforms and equipment: The soccer rules committee strongly recommends that the head referee and coach examine, as stipulated in 5-2-2d, the uniforms and equipment of each player prior to the start of the game. Give special attention to the legality and safety of the cleats.

2. Attire: It is the responsibility of each coach to insure that all players are properly attired before and during a contest.

3. Time wasting: The committee is concerned with time-wasting tactics being used by coaches to gain an advantage. Officials have the authority to stop the clock and caution coaches and players engaging in those tactics.

NCAA
Hash Marks (1-7)

The committee designated the unattached hash marks located on either side of both goals as a point of emphasis. The diagram in the rulebook showing the mark's appropriate placement will be enlarged to assist facility maintenance personnel in making the appropriate marks.

No Substitution During Corner Kicks (3-4b)

During its Feb. 1-4 meeting in Indianapolis, the NCAA men's and women's soccer rules committee revisited an old friend: substitution rules.

The committee made one small change regarding substitutions, voting to eliminate substitution opportunities on corner kicks by either team.

NCAA referees are reminded of the provisions in 3-6 that substitutes must: report to the scorer's table or nearest assistant referee, "be ready to enter the game before the time when substitutions are allowed," remain near the halfway line and be beckoned by the referee. At no time may the defensive team use a late-decided substitution to thwart an offensive attack — the substitute has to be at the table before the throw-in or goalkick stoppage. If the player reports to the table or assistant referee during the stoppage, play continues until the next substitution opportunity.

Sudden-Victory (7-1a)

The committee made an editorial change on how a game ends in overtime. The rulebook will refer to overtime periods as *"sudden-victory"* overtime periods instead of as "sudden-death" overtime periods.

Overtime Periods (7-1c)

The committee reviewed the postseason overtime procedure that allows for four 15-minute overtime periods before the game goes to a penalty-kick tiebreaker procedure. The Division I men's soccer committee requested the review in light of both 1999 Men's College Cup semifinal games being decided in the fourth overtime period.

The committee reviewed the 1999 NCAA championship games across all three divisions that went to four overtime periods. McCrath said the final decision came down to the student-athlete experience. "The committee felt that a student-athlete, given the opportunity to decide a game result on the field or go to a tiebreaker procedure, would prefer to play the overtime," McCrath said. "Accordingly, the committee decided to make no changes to the current tiebreaker procedure for postseason games."

Language is Point of Emphasis

"Once again, the committee addressed the continuing problems regarding the use of offensive, insulting or abusive language or gestures, intended or otherwise, that continue to occur in intercollegiate soccer matches. The annual report issued by the NSCAA ethics committee that monitors sportsmanship and ethical conduct confirms that the problem is continuing and, in some cases, escalating.

• Any player, coach, team official or participant listed on the official game roster who is guilty of any incidental vulgar or profane language shall be cautioned by the referee (12-14d).

• Any player, coach, team official or participant listed on the official game roster who uses offensive, insulting or abusive language shall be ejected (12-15f).

The referee does not have discretion to deviate from application of those rules."

FIFA
Advertising Near the Field of Play
(Law 1, New IFAB Decision 4)

There shall be no advertising of any kind within the technical area or within one meter from the touchline and outside the field play on the ground. Further, allow no advertising in the area between the goalline and the goal nets.

Play 1: To raise money to send their team to the State Cup, several parents got a local sporting goods store to donate $200 in exchange for their store's logo to be painted in the center circle. The referee notices the advertising before the game.

Ruling 1: The field cannot be used as described. Early arriving referees may ask to have a groundskeeper paint over the improper markings rather than cancel the game.

At the recreational level, the referee might inform the home coach or manager that he will report the matter. At the game's end, the referee reports the illegal advertising to the league and the SRA.

Number of Substitutions (Law 3)

"In *other* matches, substitutes may be used provided that:

• The teams concerned reach an agreement on a maximum number.

• The referee is informed before the match.

If the referee is not informed, or if the teams reach no agreement before the start of the match, no more than three substitutes are allowed." *Reason:* The new text gives teams flexibility in the number of substitutions permitted in friendly matches, but the previous controls regarding teams reaching agreement on the numbers and on the need for the referee to be informed before the match still remain.

USSF Advice to Referees: Consistent with existing USSF guidelines, referees on matches such as exhibition/friendly games should inquire as far ahead of time as possible regarding the exact number of permitted substitutions agreed to by both teams. Teams are strongly encouraged to determine that number as early as possible and to communicate the information no later than when the team rosters are given to the officials.

Assistant Referee's Duties (Law 6)

Two assistant referees are appointed whose duties, subject to the decision of the referee, are to indicate (only added text shown):

• When offenses have been committed whenever the assistants are closer to the action than the referee (that includes, in particular circumstances, offenses committed in the penalty area).

• Whether, at penalty kicks, the goalkeeper has moved forward before the ball has been kicked and if the ball has crossed the line.

Assistant referees are expected to give assistance to the referee when they are in a better position to see the incident, especially for incidents inside the penalty area.

It is important to understand that the specific distance from the offense is not the main criteria. The most important consideration is that the assistant referee has a better view of the incident.

Assistant referees are also expected to indicate to the referee when the goalkeeper moves forward from his goalline at a penalty kick and the ball does not enter the goal. Determine the nature of the signal to be given by the officials in prematch discussions.

USSF Advice to Referees: Standard procedures, as outlined in the *Guide to Procedures*, clearly assign initial responsibility to the assistant referee for judging goals, whether scored during play or as a result of a penalty kick.

Six Seconds (Law 12)

An indirect free kick is awarded to the opposing team if a goalkeeper inside his own penalty area:

• Takes more than six seconds while controlling the ball with his hands before releasing it from his possession. *Reason:* Time wasting by the goalkeeper with the ball in his hands or arms is now measured in time rather than distance. The Law no longer limits the goalkeeper to taking four steps when he has control of the ball in his hands or arms.

USSF Advice to Referees: In removing the "four-step rule" and now defining time wasting solely in terms of time, IFAB has moved the Law even closer to the original reason for that limitation. Referees are reminded, however, that the time taken by the goalkeeper while gaining control of the ball is not counted, trivial infringements of that limitation should not be penalized and the referee must not count the time verbally or with any visible action.

> **Play 2:** Keeper A1 catches the ball after a shot on goal. Well within the six-second time limit, A1 uses nine steps to run 15 yards with the ball and releases an overhand throw some 50 yards to A9.
>
> **Ruling 2:** Legal. Continue playing.

Gesture Listed as Send-off Offense (Law 12)

In the listing of sending-off offenses, number six now reads:

• Uses offensive, insulting or abusive language *and/or gestures. Reason:* A player may now be sent off if, in the opinion of the referee, he is guilty of using language or gestures which are offensive, insulting or abusive. The referee must take into account the severity of the offense. He continues to have the authority to decide whether, in his opinion, a player's unacceptable language or gestures are to be deemed a sending-off offense.

USSF Advice to Referees: USSF has long advised referees that the use of the term "language" in prior editions of the *Laws of the Game* was to be interpreted to include gestures. The referee must judge all verbal and nonverbal communication.

Equalize Number of Players Taking Kicks From the Penalty Mark

Two added bullet points read:

• When a team finishes the match with a greater number of players than their opponents, they shall reduce their numbers to equate with that of their opponents and inform the referee of the name and number of each player excluded. The team captain has that responsibility.

• Before the start of kicks from the penalty mark, the referee shall ensure that only an equal number of players from each team remain within the center circle and they shall take the kicks. *Reason:* The arrangement for kicks from the penalty mark is applied at the end of play when one team has fewer players on the field of play than the other because of expulsion or injury and all eligible substitutes have been used.

That is done to avert the situation in which the team with fewer players, having taken all their kicks, that team's strongest kicker would be advantaged by being matched against the weakest kicker of the team with more players.

USSF Advice to Referees: The referee will be aware of such an imbalance of numbers and must take the initiative with the affected team captain to obtain the necessary information about who will not participate in the kicks (and who must also therefore not be on the field during that activity).

Players who are off the field to correct illegal equipment or to care for bleeding or blood on the uniform are still considered players and may participate in kicks from the penalty mark, provided their return to the field follows the requirements of Law 3 (referee inspection and permission). Players off the field temporarily due to an injury may also return to the field, provided they have the referee's permission.

A player who is declared by the team captain to be injured and unable to participate in kicks from the penalty mark cannot be substituted, even if the team has a substitution remaining. In such a case, consider the team reduced in size just as if a player had been sent off. The opposing team will reduce its size by a like number.

The referee must make every effort to complete any player inspections he is required to do under Law 3 in advance of beginning to take kicks from the penalty mark.

Play 3: Team A starts the tournament semifinal game with only nine players. In a heated contest, you send off both A9 and A8. With one minute left to play, A7 suffers an ankle injury requiring him to go off the field to have the ankle taped, and you notice A6 is hobbling in pain. The game ends as a 1-1 draw, but one team must advance to the finals.

After the coin toss, captain A4 says A6 is injured and cannot take part in the kicks from the penalty mark. You notice A4 has blood on his jersey and see that A3 has a bloody knee from a contusion during a last-minute slide tackle.

Ruling 3: Inform the team B captain that only six team B shooters will be needed, and after he identifies them to you by number, all other team B players, including coaches, must depart the field. Inform A4 to change into another jersey and tell A4 that A3 must be cleaned of blood before he can participate. Before ordering the first kick, make sure A4 has switched jerseys. If A3 is still receiving medical attention, remind yourself that you must personally check A3 before he enters the field.

If all six rounds are needed to determine a winner, both keepers A1 and B1 must participate as shooters sometime during the first six kicks. The provision in Law 2 that a team must have at least seven players to start or continue a match is not in effect during the kicks from the penalty mark. A team may continue with as few as one shooter.

Chapter 5

Key Rule Differences

By Carl P. Schwartz

During your pregame discussion, you talk about certain aspects of match control. Do you ever discuss rule differences? Your ability to remember the correct ruling may be key to successful game management in a heated match.

How will you keep them straight in your mind? This chapter will help with the key rule differences.

Interscholastic and intercollegiate soccer have altered rules over the years to emphasize different aspects, such as sportsmanship, safety and differences in skill levels. Those changes will continue to be a part of the landscape for soccer officials. However, the NFHS and NCAA continue to make significant strides to more closely align their rules of competition with the FIFA *Laws of the Game*.

ADMINISTRATIVE MATTERS
Forfeits

FIFA: The referee is empowered to terminate the game because of outside interference. The referee has no power to decide that either team is disqualified and thereby the loser of the match. The referee provides the appropriate authorities with a match report. (5)

NFHS: The referee may forfeit the match if a team has fewer than seven eligible players (3-1-2). The head referee may terminate the game if conditions warrant. (5-3-2b, 5-3-1 Situation D, 5-4-1 Situation A)

NCAA: The referee may forfeit the game to the opposing team under three conditions: a coach prolongs a discussion or refuses to leave the field at the request to do so; a team without prior notification or extenuating circumstances is not on the field, prepared to play within 15 minutes of the contracted starting time; a team refuses to return to the field within three minutes after being ordered to by the referee.

Numbers on Jerseys

FIFA: There is no mention in the *Laws of the Game*. Certain competition rules may require numbered jerseys.

NFHS: All players, except for goalkeepers, must have a distinct minimum six-inch Arabic or Gothic number on the back of their jersey, and the same four-inch number on the front of their jersey or shorts. The number must be of a clearly contrasting color. (4-1-1b)

NCAA: All players, including goalkeepers, must have a distinct minimum eight-inch number on the back of their jersey, and the same four-inch number on the front of their jersey. The numbers must be easily distinguishable. (4-3)

Officiating Systems of Control

FIFA: Use a single referee. Two assistant referees may assist and advise the referee. That is the diagonal system of control. The referee keeps time on the field. A fourth official may assist the officiating team. (*Referee Administrative Handbook*; Policy of Systems of Officiating Soccer Games).

NFHS: The dual, diagonal or three-whistle system may be used. A timer keeps the time unless otherwise agreed. (5-1-1, 6-2-1)

NCAA: The diagonal system is preferred, but either the dual or the diagonal system may be used. The timer keeps the time unless there is no electronic scoreboard visible to spectators and bench areas. In this case, the referee will keep time on the field. The conference may designate an alternate official to assist. (5-1)

Overtime

FIFA: If no goals or an equal number of goals are scored, the game shall be termed a draw (10). Where tournament progression dictates a winner must be decided, play extra time if dictated by local rules, followed by kicks from the penalty mark, if needed. Only players on the field may participate in the kicks. (Kicks from the Penalty Mark) In a Law change for 2000, be sure to balance the number of kickers between the teams, if, due to injury or send offs, a team has less than 11 shooters.

NFHS: By state high school association adoption, regular-season games tied after 80 minutes may be settled in some form of tiebreaker. If the score remains tied, the game ends in a draw, unless the state association dictates a winner must be decided (7-3). Where tournament progression dictates a winner must be decided, play extra time, followed by kicks from the penalty mark, if needed. (A Sample Tournament Progression)

NCAA: Regular-season matches have two sudden-victory overtimes of 15 minutes each. If the game remains tied after two 15-minute overtime periods, it is a tie (7-1a). Teams still tied in postseason play will take kicks from the penalty mark to determine a winner. Allow all players on the official game roster to participate in a tiebreaker. Tournament or postseason progression is detailed in 7-1b.

Suspended Game, Game May Not Continue

FIFA: Not mentioned in the *Laws of the Game*. Traditionally, referees will report the circumstances (time at the suspension, score, misconduct cards, circumstances leading to the suspension) and the appropriate authorities will determine the appropriate action. Often, the action taken is a replay of the contest.

NFHS: If one complete half or more was played, the game may be declared an official game. If the teams played less than one half of the game, follow state association adoption. (7-1-3)

NCAA: A suspended game that cannot continue must be reported to the governing sports authority, which determines the next action. A contest that has reached the 70th minute may be considered a completed contest. A contest stopped before the 70th minute, and not completed at a later date, is terminated and does not count. (10-9)

Tactical Instructions/Coaching Areas

FIFA: The technical area extends one meter on either side of the seating area and to one meter from the touchline. Only one person at a time is authorized to verbally convey tactical instructions and he must return to his position immediately after giving the instructions. (3 IBD 2, 5, The Technical Area)

NFHS: Coaches or bench personnel may not use video replays. Only verbal communication to one's own team are allowed. No one may coach from outside the team area. Team areas are at least 10 feet from the touchline, starting 10 yards on each side of the halfway line for 20 yards. Caution and display a yellow card to violators. (1-5-1, 1-5-3, 12-8-1e, f)

NCAA: Only verbal communication, without aids, to one's own team are allowed. No one may coach from outside the team area. Team areas are at least 10 feet from the touchline, starting five yards on each side of the halfway line for 20 yards. For the first instance, the referee informs the coach that a repetition results in an indirect free kick for the opposing team. Another violation results in a caution to the offending coach (display the yellow card under NCAA rules) and persistent verbal harassment results in an ejection. (1-12b, 12-20)

Time of Game

FIFA: Play two 45-minute halves. The referee has discretionary power to allow for time lost due to substitution or other cause. Halftime will not exceed 15 minutes. (7)

NFHS: Play two 40-minute halves. The clock is stopped for goals, penalty kicks, cautions and disqualifications, and when the officials order it stopped. Halftime is 10 minutes. (7-1-1, 7-2-1, 7- 4-1)

NCAA: Play two 45-minute halves. The clock is stopped for goals, penalty kicks, players being cautioned or ejected, television timeouts and when the referee signals for it to be stopped. Halftime may be as long as 15 minutes. (7-1, 7-2)

Using Video Replays

FIFA: Not mentioned in the *Laws of the Game*.

NFHS: Referees are prohibited from consulting video replays to assist in any decisions. (5-1-2)

NCAA: Same as FIFA.

Field Conditions

FIFA: The referee has the power to suspend play if the field becomes unplayable and decides whether to start the match based on field conditions. (5, *Referee Administrative Handbook* 3037)

NFHS: The host school shall decide whether the field and other conditions are suitable for starting the match. Once the match begins and until it ends, the referee shall judge whether the match may be safely continued. (1-7-1)

NCAA: Same as FIFA. (5-3, 5-5a AR 8, 10-9)

Field Markings

FIFA: The use of a hashmark, 10 yards from the corner arc, off the field of play and at right angles to the goalline is optional. (1, IFAB 5)

NFHS: Same as FIFA. (1-2-10)

NCAA: The hashmark is mandatory. "Penalty: The game shall not begin and may result in forfeiture by the home team to be determined by the governing sports authority." (1-7)

FOULS AND MISCONDUCT CARDS
Goalkeepers Changing Places

FIFA: If a field player and the goalkeeper exchange jerseys during play, without notifying the referee before making the change, play continues until a natural stoppage in play. At that next stoppage, both players are cautioned. Those are mandatory cautions. (3, *The Eight Mandatory Cautions 1999*)

NFHS: If a field player and the goalkeeper exchange jerseys during play, without notifying the referee before making the change, both players receive a verbal warning at the next stoppage. (3-5-1 Penalty)

NCAA: Same as NFHS. (3-7 Penalty)

Stooping

FIFA: Not mentioned in the *Laws of the Game*.

NFHS: Players may not stoop in front of or behind

opponents in such a way as to cause a fall or loss of balance. Award a direct free kick. (12-1-2)

NCAA: Players may not bend over in front of or behind opponents in such a manner as to cause a fall or loss of balance. Award a direct free kick. (12-1 AR 1)

Stopping the Clock

FIFA: Do not stop the clock to administer misconduct cards. (5) Referees, at their discretion, may add time to the end of the playing period for all time lost. (7)

NFHS: Stop the clock while issuing a misconduct card. (6-2-3a)

NCAA: Same as NFHS. (6-3b-4)

Who May Be Carded?

FIFA: Only card a player or named substitute. A player red carded before the match may be replaced. A player sent off during the match may not be replaced. (3)

NFHS: Players, coaches and bench personnel may be cautioned or disqualified. A yellow and red card disqualification ("soft red" i.e., the player may be replaced) is issued for taunting, excessive celebration or a subsequent caution. A team can't substitute for a player who is disqualified during a period of play, but the team may replace a player who is red carded during halftime. (12-8-1, 12-8-2, 12-8-3)

NCAA: Players, coaches and bench personnel may be cautioned or ejected. A player ejected before the match may be replaced. (12-14 through 12-17)

PLAYERS AND SUBSTITUTIONS
Captains

FIFA: No mention in the *Laws of the Game*. Traditionally, the coach appoints a team leader to act as a conduit for information between the referee and the team. Traditionally, the visiting captain calls to coin toss. The team losing the coin toss will kick off to start the match. (8)

NFHS: Each team shall designate a captain, who serves as the team representative, gets essential information or addresses an official for an interpretation (3-1-1 a, b, c). The visiting team captain shall call the coin toss while the coin is in the air. The winner may chose to defend a goal or have the kickoff. (5-2-2e-2)

NCAA: Team captains may wear a special armband to distinguish themselves (4-1c). The visiting team captain shall call the coin toss. The winner may chose to defend a goal or have the kickoff. (8-1, AR 1)

Rosters

FIFA: Give player and substitute names to the referee before the match. Nominate between three and seven substitutes, based on competition rules (3). If the competition rules require the names of the substitutes to be given to the referee prior to the match, failure to submit the roster of eligible names means that no substitutes can be permitted. (3)

NFHS: Each coach shall submit a team roster to the officials at least five minutes before the match (3-1-3). Players may be added to the roster after the start of play. (3-1-3 Situation B)

NCAA: The names of players, coaches and bench personnel and a list of each player's total cautions and ejection's must be given to the scorekeeper no later than 15 minutes before game time (3-2a). Players not listed on the game roster are not eligible to play (3-2b).

Substitutes

FIFA: Allow between three and seven substitutes, subject to the rules of each league. A replaced player may not play in the game again (3). A 1999 law change allows reentry in youth, veteran and women's games. Remove an injured player as soon as possible, given game conditions. It is not necessary to replace that player. (3, 5)

NFHS: No limits on the number of substitutes or reentries (3-3-1). An injured player that is attended to on the field "shall leave the field and may be replaced." (3-3-2a)

NCAA: No limits on the number of substitutes, but players are allowed no reentry in the first half, one reentry in the second half, no reentry within the same overtime period. Allow the goalkeepers unlimited reentry as long as they reenter as goalkeepers. An injured player may be substituted for and reenter in any period if the injury was caused by an opposing player who was cautioned or ejected in connection with the injury. A player required to leave because of blood and the substitute are not charged with a substitution. (3-5)

When to Allow Substitutions

FIFA: Allow substitutions when play has been stopped after the player being replaced has left the field (3). The referee shall be informed of the proposed substitution before it is made. The substitute enters at the halfway line (3). *Editor's note: There are many differences at the local youth level. Be sure to check local variations for the competition you are working.*

NFHS: Either team may substitute between periods, on a

goalkick, when a goal is scored, when an injured player is attended to on the field, when a player is cautioned or when a player is disqualified. Teams gaining possession of the ball may substitute on a throw-in or corner kick. For entry on a throw-in, goalkick or corner kick, the substitute must have reported to the scorer before the dead ball. The substitute must remain at the scorer's table. The substitute shall remain at the table until an official beckons the substitute onto the field (3-4-1a). Coach's instructions shall not be given to players of either team when coaches or medics attend to an injured player (3-3-1, 3-3-2, 3-3-2a, 3-4-1).

NCAA: Either team may substitute on a goalkick, when a goal is scored, when a player is ordered off for an equipment change or between periods. If a team substitutes for a player who is ordered off the field for an equipment change, the opposing team may replace an equal number of players at that time. In case of an injury or a cautioned player, only the injured or cautioned player may be replaced, with the opposing team allowed to replace an equal number of players.

Teams may substitute on their own throw-ins. However, the opposing team may do so only if the team in control of the restart substitutes. Substitutes must have reported to the scorer's table and be beckoned by the referee before entering the field. (3-4)

Signals

FIFA: There are seven signals mandated for use by the referee. They are advantage, corner kick, direct free kick, goalkick, indirect free kick, misconduct card and penalty kick. All three codes agree there are seven signals used by assistant referees. They are corner kick, goalkick, offside-far, offside-near, offside-middle, substitution and throw-in. (Signals by the Referee, Signals by the Assistant Referee from the 1997 edition of the *Laws of the Game*)

NFHS: The NFHS rulebook also mandates the use of a timeout signal (wrists crossed above your head), offside signal (hands on hips) and goal scored (timeout signal followed by pointing to the center circle). (NFHS Official Soccer Signals)

NCAA: The NCAA rulebook mandates the use of the timeout signal, in addition to those used by FIFA. (Official Referee's Signals)

Suspension of Play

FIFA: After a temporary suspension of play for any reason not mentioned in the Laws, the restart is a dropped ball. (8)

NFHS: After a temporary suspension of play for any reason not mentioned in the rules, restart the game with an indirect free kick by the team clearly in possession. If there was no clear possession, restart play with a dropped ball between two opposing players. (9-3-1)

NCAA: Restart the game with an indirect free kick by the team clearly in possession. If there was no clear possession, restart play with a dropped ball. (9-3b)

Throw-ins

All codes agree on certain elements: the thrower may not score directly from a throw-in; the thrower must face the field of play; have part of both feet on the ground on or behind the touchline; deliver the ball from over and behind the head; the thrower may not play the ball twice in succession; the throw must be taken from the location where the ball crossed the touchline; and the ball is in play as soon as any part of the ball breaks the plane above any part of the touchline.

FIFA: FIFA only says that the thrower must use both hands (15). *Advice to Referees 15.3* allows a player who lacks the normal use of one or both hands to perform a legal throw-in if the ball is delivered over the head. *"There is no requirement in law 15 prohibiting spin or rotational movement.* Referee must judge the correctness of the throw-in solely on the basis of law 15."

NFHS: In addition, the thrower must "use both hands with equal force … in one continuous movement" (15-1-2). In a rule change for 2000, if the ball does not enter play, award the opposing team a throw-in from the previous location. (15-1-5)

NCAA: The thrower "shall use both hands equally." (15-2)

Chapter 6

The Pregame Conference: The 10 Most Critical Minutes in Soccer

By David L. Keller

Regardless of the level of play, the pregame conference between referees and assistant referees is critical to successful soccer officiating. It is not enough for the referee to know the Laws and count on the assistant referees to call the ball in and out of play. In the diagonal system of control, the three officials must act as a team. The beginning of team building is the pregame conference.

How thorough should it be? What should be covered? Ten minutes is a minimum, longer if the referees want to discuss team tendencies and strategy.

The topics covered should include the following in a logical and comfortable order.

Referee Responsibilities

The referee indicates the diagonal he plans to run. Unless designated by the assignor, designate a senior assistant referee to take the referee's duties if the referee is incapacitated. The senior assistant referee runs next to the technical area and will have primary responsibility for handling substitutes and controlling coach, technical personnel and substitute behavior. If the referee expects the assistants to be in any position not specified in the *Guide to Procedures*, cover that. Referees should remind the assistant referees that they should stay with the second-to-last defender and must follow the ball to the goalline. Identify backup timekeeping and scoring responsibilities.

Set Plays

Cover positioning on set plays, especially variations from the *Guide to Procedures*.

Throw-ins

Insure the proper spot for the throw-in. Usually assistant referees watch for infractions of the feet and the referee will watch the throw itself. If the referee considers most throw-in shortcomings trifling, that should be covered. The players expect consistency.

Goalkicks

Most referees expect the assistant to quickly check ball placement then move to the second-to-last defender. Some want the assistant referee to move to the edge of the penalty area to make certain the ball clears. (That is usually limited to youth games or unusual circumstances.) Positions may change based on who takes the kick.

Corner Kicks

The assistant referee should be behind the ball and on the goalline on corner kicks taken on the assistant's side. If the boundaries don't permit that positioning, the referee and assistant referee should agree on positioning *before* the contest. For kicks opposite the assistant, some NFHS referees prefer the assistant referee move into the field, usually to the intersection of the penalty area and the goalline to judge ball position relative to the goal and goalline. USSF guidance on far-corner corner kicks is to stand just behind the near corner flagpost. The referee must discuss what is expected.

Penalty Kicks

It is critical to discuss penalty kick procedures before the match. Normally the assistant referee will move to the intersection of the penalty area and the goalline and has primary responsibility for judging a goal. Referees differ on other responsibilities. Assistant referees watch for goalkeeper movement. Work out a signal to communicate there was unfair movement. Some referees want assistants to watch for encroachment. It is a team effort to control a penalty kick.

Free Kicks

Free kicks near the penalty area have a strong goal-scoring opportunity and deserve pregame coverage. The refereeing team must cover the wall, offside position and the goalline. Referees may set the wall and move to cover offside and expect the assistant to cover the goalline. In many cases, offensive and defensive players together in the wall are the most critical element. Whatever the positioning, the responsibilities and appropriate signals should be discussed.

Foul Recognition

Expecting assistant referees to call fouls under certain specified conditions is becoming more important and is key to effective use of the diagonal system of control. Referees should specifically encourage assistant referees to signal fouls or misconduct which could not be seen by the referee. The old limitation of "… Let me call them in the penalty area" should be avoided. Due to the 1995-96 Law change, communications when advantage is given or withdrawn should be discussed.

Offside

Emphasize that the assistant referees call only offside and not offside position. The primary discussion should be participation in the play and how much of a time interval the referee is expecting to see from the assistants before flagging offside. Players and spectators object when the assistant referee "calls it too late." Finally, the referee should cover a signal for acknowledging an offside flag when no stoppage results.

Goals Scored

Referees should not award a goal until they have confirmed it with the assistant referee (while you're at it, why not double-check *both* assistants). In the pregame, the referee should remind the assistant referees to acknowledge a successful goal by sprinting upfield without arm signals.

Disputed Goal

Generally, referees prefer no flag signal if the assistant referee disputes a possible goal. The *Guide to Procedures* directs the assistant to remain stationary and at attention if the attacking team committed a foul or a player other than the scorer was offside. On the other hand, if the flag was raised for offside by the player who scored, keep the flag up and treat the offside infraction like any non-scoring situation. Communications are critical. Cover those vital points in the pregame.

Signals

In addition to the USSF-approved assistant referee signals, nearly every referee has signals or clues they use. Those must be covered in detail in the pregame and include:

Acknowledgment. Some referees use eye contact to acknowledge a signal by the assistant. Others may use a hand signal such as thumbs-up or a head nod. Regardless, that acknowledgment is critical for good communications and rapport between officials.

Attention getting. An assistant referee may need to confer with the referee during the match. A clear signal between assistant and referee is critical, usually a hand over the patch or the flag held across the body parallel to the ground.

Foul location. If the referee was caught downfield on a quick counterattack, and needs help to determine if the foul was inside or outside the penalty area, the *Guide to Procedures* recommends the flag move to between the legs if the assistant referee judges a defensive foul occurred in the penalty area. The flag remains outside the leg if the infraction occurred outside the penalty area. That signal is given only if requested.

Restart after a foul. For indirect free kick restarts, one potential signal is to follow the directional signal by placing the flag straight up. Other agreed upon signals are appropriate.

Mirroring Signals

Remind assistant referees to mirror signals if the referee's vision of a flag is obscured. Mirroring is particularly important during substitutions and misconduct. What should the assistants do (aside from mirroring) if the referee does not see a flag for offside, ball in touch or a foul? How long should the assistants hold the flag? Under what circumstances should the flag be dropped without acknowledgment?

Pregame and Postgame Activities

Entering and leaving the field as a team and participation in the postgame handshake should be covered. Discuss pregame activities. Determine if the referee expects the assistant referees to conduct the player inspection. The pregame activities will also vary. Many referees prefer the assistants accompany them to the center prior to the game then trot to inspect the net, remain to greet the goalkeeper, move to the touchline, count players and unfurl the flag to indicate readiness. Give other special instructions in the pregame. All pregame and postgame activities should support the officiating team concept.

Tactical and Strategic Considerations

If the referee or assistant referees have knowledge of players or team tendencies, discuss those before the game. The use of an offside trap or an unusual player tendency, good or bad, should be identified and any special instructions should be included.

The pregame conference allows the referee to effectively communicate expectations to the assistant referees while developing the officiating team. It permits the team to anticipate situations and provide a cohesive approach to the match insuring a fun, fair and safe environment. The conference is the most important 10 minutes during the day.

(David Keller lives in Chicago. He referees soccer at the youth, high school and collegiate levels. He is an advanced (Grade 1) instructor for the American Youth Soccer Organization and serves as director of instruction for AYSO Section 6, covering Ill., Wis., Iowa and Minn.)

Chapter 7

Holders of the Golden Thread

By Carl P. Schwartz and Joseph S. Blatter

There was a time that soccer was played without officials. The two teams just went out and played the game. In the English parks and schoolyards, the "gentlemanly" captains would call their own fouls or admit that one player on their side committed a violation. The restart would be given to the other team. Sometimes that led to "discussions" among the captains.

Eventually, a single referee was asked to sit slightly off the field and one captain or the other would "refer" a matter to the official and a decision would be rendered by the referee.

In due time, the referee stepped onto the field and ran among the players to get first hand information. At that point, the referee initiated calls for fouls and violations. However, many players still think they need to point out an opponent's misdeeds.

Competition

Growing competition calls for more from referees. There has been much talk recently about the "Modern Game" of soccer, a concept intended to recognize that soccer has been amplified with the present-day influences of competition, money, recognition, contracts, stadia and power. But at the bottom line of all those influences is money. Superstar players attract spectators into the stands. Winning major competitions (UEFA Cup, F.A. Cup) allows clubs to buy contracts of great players. Players want an increasing amount of those dollars (and pounds and drachma and yen). But around all those influences are referees who make the best decisions they are capable of given their training, fitness and ability to see and use the information provided by their refereeing partners.

Golden Thread

Longtime referees refer to those great persons who are the holders of the golden thread — the fabric that weaves the game together around the world and over time. While there are historians who study the past, and spectators who can recite starting lineups from long-forgotten World Cup teams, generally it is referees who study the spirit of the game. Generally it is referees who devote hours and hours to the study of the history of the *Laws of the Game,* who delve into the intricacies of the interpretations. While some spectators can get a percentage of the proper interpretations right, it is generally referees who know the game's right from wrong.

Is that to say that each one of Germany's 17,000 referees could score 100 percent on a test? No. Is that to say that each of the U.S.'s 110,000 referees could act as a rules interpreter with equal effectiveness? Never a thought. But a select few referees (and some few players, coaches and administrators) are holders of the golden thread of the game. They understand the rationale behind each rule change. They have researched the history behind each rule change. They can offer an explanation to a referee (or coach or player) who asks about an interpretation.

(continued on page 74)

BACK TO THE BASICS

So much of our time at FIFA has been consumed in recent months with discussions about transfer regulations and other administrative issues that I sometimes fear that we may be in danger of losing sight of our true raison d'être.

So it was particularly refreshing to attend this year's International Football Association Board meeting, where the subject is always the *Laws of the Game* and therefore has the welcome effect of concentrating our thoughts on what really matters most: the game itself.

For let's never forget that if the game of soccer, as played on a field by 22 players and a referee, is not healthy, then all the peripheral activities that have grown up alongside the game cannot prosper either.

With the good of the game at heart, the Board came to grips, for instance, with the growing problem of players who themselves come to grips too frequently with their opponents, holding and pulling and generally breaking the natural flow of play. An increased number of television cameras and innovative angles have revealed what the referee cannot always see, as players grapple with each other and tug at each other's shirts — maybe not least a consequence of today's trend for loose-fitting jerseys which make them that much more tempting to grab.

But it has got to stop. Soccer is played with the feet and not — with all respect to the goalkeepers — with the hands.

Meanwhile, the Board also showed its more human face by easing its instructions to referees with regard to players who almost automatically strip off their shirts to celebrate a goal. Ironically, within minutes of the Board deciding to tell referees to lighten up, at a major match not so many miles from where the Board met, a player was sent off with a second yellow card for exactly that offense, risking missing an F.A. Cup semifinal as the highlight of his career.

It is not hard to sympathize with referees who may sometimes be unsure about the messages they receive on how to deal with situations like that. A foul is a foul is a foul, one may say (although it is really never quite as clear as that), but there are also those countless other incidents that leave everything up to the referee's sense of judgment.

The work of the International Board is to try to simplify those messages and to standardize the referee's responses. But the dynamics of our sport are such that it constantly throws up new situations, and no two matches, no two players, no two incidents and no two referees are really alike.

And that just shows why soccer is the world's favorite game.

— *Written by Joseph S. Blatter*

They are the top instructors; they are the top assessors. They are referees who rose to the top levels of competition, either within a nation or internationally. Referees such as the USSF manager of referee development and education, Alfred Kleinaitis, recently selected to be a FIFA instructor, are holders of the golden thread. The great Ken Aston is another.

Rethinking

Sometimes a rule change or other change to the *Laws of the Game* has unforeseen consequences. Sometimes that rule must be altered or written off the books. One perfect example is taking the shirts off in celebrating a goal. (See Joseph S.

Blatter's thoughts on that subject in the sidebar.) Within the U.S., that problem is compounded. While the international game will now relax its standards on shirt removal, it is doubtful that rulemakers at the interscholastic level will relax that restriction — it would be inappropriate given that part of the high school experience is to develop character and sportsmanship.

Points of Emphasis

Referees officiate the game based on the Laws and rules. Everyone reading this book knows at least one or two current referees who have managed to continue refereeing without reading the rulebook, attending a clinic or association meeting. But the game is changing. Not only the rules, but also the points of emphasis. The NCAA wants a particularly strong emphasis placed on vulgar language — zero tolerance, even for an incidental use of foul language. If a referee goes one or two years and doesn't attend training sessions to gain a greater understanding of those interpretations, rule changes and points of emphasis, he is not keeping the golden thread whole.

Expressing Concern

Neither FIFA nor the USSF issues annual points of emphasis. Periodically, they do express concern that certain aspects of the game are not being whistled correctly. One recent example is tackling from behind which endangers the safety of an opponent. It was not being whistled and enforced properly when issued as a Law change. A part of the problem was with the popular press and spectators who heard only the words "tackle from behind." Those folks, who aren't keepers of the golden thread, expected a red card for every instance of a tackle from behind. That has never been the interpretation at any level of the game. A tackle from behind may not be misconduct — conceivably it may not even be a foul. More likely, less skilled players who tackle from behind will do so recklessly. If that is the case, the proper remedy is a caution. In those instances where the tackle is done with excessive force, a red card is called for. Only in those cases where the tackle from behind endangers the safety of an opponent does the referee lose the right to issue a lesser penalty — the International Football Association Board wants the referee to issue a red card.

Textile Testers

Joseph Blatter, FIFA's president, called the 1998 World Cup, the competition of textile testers. Players relentlessly grabbed opponents' shirts. Referees were used to see holding, but never with the scope as at the 1998 World Cup.

But with all the attendant publicity about holding shirts, referees around the globe are not calling that foul when it disrupts attractive, attacking soccer. So, as a part of the 2001 Memorandum, USSF and FIFA expressed their concern to you — to the referees you teach, to the referees you assess, to the referees in your association — to add a misconduct card to that foul when it puts the opponent at a disadvantage. Going beyond that plea in the rules, President Blatter wrote a personal plea in the 4/01 issue of *FIFA News*. The front-page editorial (see sidebar) makes it personal. His words — "But it has got to stop."

Grab a piece of the golden thread. Be a leader. Make the call. Mentor less experienced referees and explain the rationale as to how a few calls of holding early in the game might open the game and create a flowing atmosphere for attractive soccer.

Years to Come

Tackling from behind which endangers the safety of an opponent. Holding an opponent's jersey. Those are points of emphasis or concerns now. As a reader of a text at this level, you are either one of the people holding the golden thread or want to be holding it. Become a leader. Attend your required training. Find out what is important to the leaders of our sport — whether it is for the international game, the NCAA or NFHS. Do what they request. If you cannot abide by their rules or edits, do not whistle at that level.

The game will not go back to an official sitting on the touchline as the captains "refer" disputes to the official. The modern game is here to stay. Referees, whether professional referees or not, need to adapt as the game changes, as the influences on the game change, as the tactics being taught to players change. Stay in touch with the game as it changes. Teach others about those changes — whether it is from the front of a room as an instructor, interpreter or association training officer, or whether it is individually as an assessor or mentor.

Chapter 8

Patterns

By Carl P. Schwartz

What do the following words have in common? Life. Shed. Sonic. Void. Polka. Sofa. Role. Sponge. Song. Upon. Zone. See the last page of this chapter for the answer.

As referees, you have to spot the patterns. Intuitively, you will spot a few simple patterns. A7 will take all the team A throw-ins and heave a 40-yard throw. Slow-footed defender B3 does not have the soccer skills to dribble or make an accurate pass, so every time B3 hits the ball it will be a booming ball. Top referees read the patterns and take actions to improve their game management. Your control will improve as you sense the patterns forming, *walk* to make positioning changes based on those patterns and anticipate players' actions based on those patterns. Do not anticipate the call — anticipate the action and be ready to make the call.

If you played the game, or have extensive experience around the game as a parent or coach, you may see some of the more complex patterns. You may see the defensive leader of a flat-back four call for an offside trap and time it nicely. You may see a midfielder start an overlapping run and not get the ball directly from the player with the ball — it always comes from a one-touch pass on the second pass.

Patterns of Play

Why is it important that you pick up on that pattern? If you don't know that second pass will be to the moving midfielder A6, you are *standing* flat-footed watching an innocent five-yard pass from A8 to A10. By the time A10 strikes that one-touch pass to A6, you are motionless, 20 yards away from a sprinting A6. By the time you get up to a jog to follow play, you are 30-35 yards from play, A6 is nearing the penalty area and keeper B1, who did see the pattern forming, is running toward A6. You are *sprinting* just as you need to be stopped to see the play most clearly.

So you are 30 yards from play having to guess whether it's a penalty kick, foul by offensive player A6, contact with no foul or no contact. If you had picked up the pattern earlier, you would start *walking* as soon as you saw A6 start the overlapping run. You would be on the move, 10-15 yards behind A6 and be making the minor adjustments to get the proper angle to see B1 and A6. Based on that vastly improved positioning, you are able to sell the call — no matter what your decision.

If you find yourself *standing*, then *sprinting* and still taking some heat for your decisions, you need to work with a mentor or senior referee to spot the patterns. Working as an assistant, ask your referee what patterns she has picked up in the first half and see if you can spot those same patterns in the second half as they begin to take shape. Watch the referee make those minor positioning changes as the patterns start to form.

Let's look at one other pattern of play introduced in the second paragraph. Since slow-footed B3 is hoofing every ball he touches some 50 yards, do you need to *sprint* 50 yards upfield as soon as the ball is kicked? As always, you have to read the pattern. Under most circumstances, B3 is just clearing the ball to momentarily relieve the pressure on his goal, the ball will go to a team A player and a couple of passes later, the ball will be right back near where you *walked* to position yourself on your diagonal. There is no need to run 40 yards upfield and then run 40 yards back downfield if opponents aren't going to contest for the ball.

But suppose the team B coach has also noticed that pattern, and is playing a 4-4-2 formation. The coach tells B3 to always kick to the right third of the field as he hoofs it 50 yards. If the coach also positions both attacking players in that right third of the field, there is now a chance for a team B player to gather the long pass and start a two-on-two attack. Then you have to go.

Only by reading play, and seeing the team tendencies as the ball is in play, can you make smart positioning decisions.

Patterns in the Restarts

Let's look at the other scenario we introduced in paragraph two. Does A7 heave a 40-yard throw because he can, or does A7 heave it to the head of A9 who knows to stand exactly 40 yards away, expecting to flick the ball on to far-side attacker A11? Those two scenarios present two different positioning choices for you.

In the former (long heave because he can), you should stay deep (toward the midfield line) and start *walking* away from your assistant as team B begins a likely counterattack. Far too many athletes and coaches think a long throw is effective. Most times it is not — the ball goes to the other team and they play a possession or counterattacking style. So A7's long throw leads to team B possession and you are already on your diagonal, away from your now-lead assistant, as you transition down the field. As always, there is a chance the ball could fall nicely for team A and you might have to sprint to get into a better position. But you are playing the percentages. Plus, you have your assistant to help in those rare cases.

If you've seen the teams before and know A7 is going to heave the ball on most throw-ins, tell both assistants what you plan to do and they will be ready for your positioning and know when they will need to help. If you don't discover that trend until midway through the first half, talk to them at halftime.

But let's suppose A7's long throw has a purpose. Time after time, the tall A9 is perfectly positioned 41 yards from the thrower and as the throw is airborne, A9 checks over his shoulder to see where A11 is standing and makes minor changes to get under the throw. A simple flick-header into the path of the moving A11 and there is a chance for a shot on goal or a defender making a challenge on A11. The first incident (defender and A9 going up for an airborne ball) and the second incident (A11's shot or A11 and a closing defender) will be about 20 yards apart and happen within one second of one another. If you missed the pattern and are *standing* between A7 and A9, you are 40 yards away from where A11's shot is going to take place and will have to *sprint* to get a decent look at play.

If you picked up what's going to happen, as A7 retrieves the ball to make the throw, you *walk* to the dropping zone (90 degrees from where the A9 versus defender challenge will take place). Knowing to expect the flick-header, you get into the dropping zone to make sure A9 doesn't use his elbows on the way up or that the defender doesn't push A9 in the back. Seeing no foul as they both ascend, you've shifted your weight and maybe even taken a step or two toward A11. You *walk* three steps toward A11 as the ball rolls toward A11 and you are perfectly positioned, 10-15 yards from either the shot or the contested ball. Should there be a foul, you are close enough to sell your call. Your head was steady as you viewed the play; you weren't sprinting at top speed at a critical viewing time.

One More

When a team has a direct free kick opportunity from 20-25 yards from goal, what does that team do in the wall? Do they even put a player in the wall?

Some teams consciously spread the field — each player moving 10-12 yards from each teammate. That compounds the defender's problems because each defender must mark up against a specific opponent. The team taking the restart can do a long chip, a short chip, a direct shot on goal near side, a direct shot on goal far side and there are players there to poach a deflection or rebound from the woodwork or keeper. Unfortunately, that compounds your problems too, since you have to guess who the attacking team is going to hit the restart toward. Did you read that the tallest player moved from deep in the defense and is now one of the players at the far post, like the U.S. national team used to do with Alexi Lalas in the late '90s? That's a good place to *walk* toward for an anticipated restart.

How about when attackers get into the wall? Do they illegally push and shove to gain their preferred position? Since the ball isn't in play, it can't be a foul — it has to be incidental contact or misconduct. That's a good time for some preventive officiating. *Walk* there. Sometimes the defenders see the attackers coming and push to keep them out of the wall, or at least away from a preferred position. Again — incidental or misconduct, but prevent it by getting there. Learn each team's tendencies early in the game and make your positioning changes.

Patterns in Substitutions

Twenty-five minutes into the game you have everything under control. You know A7 is going to take the long throw, B3 is hoofing every ball to both attacking players and A5 and B8 are going to hassle each other on every wall. That's OK — just 25 people having fun.

But now you see your fourth official or bench-side assistant calling for a substitution. Will A13's influence on the game change anything? For the first minute or two, you may want to position yourself a step or two closer to A13, no matter where the ball is, than you normally would. Watch intently. During stoppages, *walk* on a path that takes you nearer A13 as you transition to your next restart position. Is A13 speedy and crafty and more willing to take on defenders with a dribble than A8 who went out? Is A13 about 20 pounds overweight and trying to throw that weight around the first time he tries to get into a wall? It may take better positioning to see that. It may take some player management skills that weren't needed during the first 25 minutes. It may take some preventive officiating. It may take a card. A13, and all the other subs that report into the game, have to blend into the atmosphere you and the players created in the early stages of the game. Otherwise there is chaos. If your game management, foul decisions and misconduct choices bend with each substitution, you lose the consistency that is asked for by players and coaches.

Patterns of Misbehavior

For dozens of different reasons, players engage in unsporting behavior. Perhaps they are unskilled at the competitive level they are playing — a U-13 youngster trying to play up in a U-16 league. Perhaps A2 just got told he's failing in school and is

going to take out some of that anger on team B shins. There is
the possibility B5 played on team A for three years, and this is
the first time she's competing against former teammates.

Those are tough to read. You can get a sense of some of that
in pregame warmups. Watch who is talking to whom. Listen for
angry responses when a coach addresses a player from a
distance.

More likely, the misconduct pattern you will pick up will be
persistent infringement. *Referee* has written about the two types
of persistent infringement — A4 repeatedly fouling a series of
team B players or numerous team B players picking on star
player A10. You have to catch both of those patterns. Some
(admittedly not many) referees write the jersey number of
players who are called for a foul on their hands — white team
on the right hand, blue team on the left hand. Effective, but
sloppy.

Not as efficient is simply verbally saying the jersey number
of the player who you judge committed a foul. It may just be a
whisper to yourself: "That's the second time I've called one
against A6." Or it may be loud enough for the player to hear:
"Careful eight, that's the third one on you." *Hint:* If you are
going to say it loud enough for the player who committed the
foul to hear it, say it loud enough for both the player who
fouled and the player who was fouled to hear it. As you
transition to your next restart position, walk on a line that takes
you near those players. There is a small psychological edge
there — the fouled player gains a slight feeling of being more
protected.

Patterns of Touches

Players' styles lead to your being able to protect them in various ways. In the example at the beginning of the chapter, A10 played one-touch balls to a streaking A6. As a referee, you can protect a player playing one-touch soccer. Let's suppose that in A10's first five touches of the ball, an opponent hits A10 three times. You should have blown at least two fouls against team B, or called out, "Play on" loudly a couple of times.

But if B9 dribbles the length of the field a few of times, or takes on four defenders in an attempt to get into the penalty area, and has 75 touches on the ball, B9 may get hit two or three times by opponents. That's natural, to be expected and a part of the game. If a defender is in the immediate vicinity of the ball and lightly thumps a shinguard now and again, it sounds like that defender is playing the game the way it should be played. That action isn't careless. That action isn't reckless. Those are the criteria for a foul.

Patterns of Time

Some teams play a possession game. Other teams play a counterattacking style. Other teams fall into a defensive shell. Those styles shift based on the players' ability, players' fitness, the score and the time remaining in the game. A possession team down one goal in the last three minutes of the game is going to have a vastly different style in those last three minutes than in the first 87 minutes. You have to make the adjustments — at a time when you've been running hard for 87 minutes.

You have to have the mental clarity to bring to the forefront all those patterns you've seen earlier in the game. That demands physical fitness. It demands hydration — with as little as two-percent dehydration, you lose the focus needed to make crisp decisions. It demands a comfort level with your surroundings. If you have a tendency to have great first halves but struggle in the second half, you are in over your head — move down one competitive level. Or, stay at that level, but get the added confidence of having your mentor or a senior referee on your line.

The pattern of time does not simply extend to within the context of a single game. It may be the time within a competition — semifinals are more intense than pool play. For league play, it may get more intense as the season progresses. If team A loses today, the game you are refereeing, they are mathematically eliminated from the championship, even though there are three weeks left in the season. They know that. You should too. You will be a better referee when all those factors are known.

Patterns of Geography

A foul is a foul is a foul. Sort of. If the ball is in play, and the action is on the field and the contact is with an opponent (or the ball in the case of handling), a careless action is a foul. A reckless action is a foul and misconduct. The mere fact that A3 held an opponent, whether he meant to or not, is a foul. The mere fact that B11 made contact with A6 before the ball while tackling for the ball is a foul. Sometimes the action will be deemed trifling based on the competitive level. Sometimes a legitimate foul will not be whistled because of an advantage situation. All that is called foul sorting.

But several types of geography play a role in your call sorting. Let's start with global geography. British and Scandinavian players use a lot of upper-body jostling as they contest for a ball. Perhaps because of wet fields and uncertain rolls, players from that area of the world use the long ball and crosses into the mixer to score. They are adept at playing in the air. They grew up with a little jostling as they go up for a ball. If you whistle a game involving two teams from that area (say at an international youth tournament like the USA Cup or you travel to Europe for one of their youth tournaments), they will be confused by your whistle if you don't adapt to their style of play.

Similarly, most players on teams from Brazil or Central America learned to play on hard city streets and tight alleys. Quick, short passes are the norm. Those players don't want defenders nicking their heels or coming up over the ball. There is a move called la plancha, or a defender driving the leg from knee height toward the instep of the player with the ball, cleats exposed. A referee's game control could balance on a single no-call of a la plancha. If you are going to referee teams from those areas, speak with a mentor or senior referee, learn to spot the foul and enforce what is culturally correct.

Mixing Geography

What do you do when you have team tendencies that don't match? Team patterns are divergent? How does a German referee balance the overly physical upper-body play of an English team against the artistic technical skill of a Brazilian team that can make 20 passes in a 10-yard area? That is where call sorting becomes vital. You must balance the scales to make the playing field as level as possible. The English players have been playing that way since early childhood, so to totally take away every upper-body challenge would put them at a severe disadvantage. Likewise, the Brazilians must expect an occasional thump on the shinguard if they touch the ball 30 times in a row without a foul being whistled. At the outset, you must keep the game safe, enjoyable and fair. It is a delicate balance to mix geographic styles. It's hard. That's why it's typically FIFA referees who have that problem. But so do you. When you go to State Cup, you have one U-15 team coached by someone who learned to play in England. A former Guatemalan national team player coaches their cross-state rival. You've got their game in 20 minutes.

Geography on the Field

As many times as I've read the *Laws of the Game*, I've not seen the paragraph that explains that for a referee to call a penalty kick, it's got to be "a good 'un." There is no level of seriousness, or degree of severity, associated with a penalty kick. A major foul committed by a defender within the penalty area leads to a penalty kick restart. In concept, simple. In reality, you want to set some balance for the players. While it would be simplistic to say you wouldn't want seven penalty kicks in a game, that wouldn't happen because the players would realize you are calling it that tight and make the needed adjustments. But you would have taken a lot of that game. Players would be playing in fear. They would know they couldn't foul inside the area, so there would be many more, and much more severe, fouls outside the area, before the team could work the ball into the penalty area.

There are also a few areas on the field where a careless foul might be considered more — simply because of its location. For any foul right in front of a team bench, you might want to process this question: "Should I give a card for that one?" Why? There is no tactical reason for a foul 50-60 yards from the goalline. What message is the fouling player trying to send? I can intimidate my opponent? I can brutalize my opponent, even right in front of his teammates, and nothing will happen to me? My team isn't playing so well, so maybe I can fire them up with a little hard contact right in front of the benches? (By the way, that's a great tactic in NHL hockey. But you better be thinking yellow card if you see it in your games above the U-14 level.)

For much the same reason, fouls tight to the corner flagposts or fouls within a few yards of the midfield line should be seen as more aggressive than fouls in the attacking third. There is no tactical reason for the foul — so look for the hidden agenda. Sense the pattern. Was it the team enforcer getting even for contact you didn't call? Was it a substitute who hasn't yet adapted to the tone you set early in the game?

Constant Motion

If you find yourself *standing*, then *sprinting* and still taking some heat for your decisions, you need to work with a mentor or senior referee to spot the patterns. Older referees, perhaps even the one you call, "Center Circle Charley," have often learned the technique of constant motion. Read the patterns, sense where the next significant action is going to take place and walk in that direction. As the play is a second away from forming, make any needed adjustment to get a clear angle on the play, then freeze your head so your vision is clearly focused. Top referees have learned to read the patterns on almost every play. Their positioning is better. Their ability to sell calls is better. Their game management techniques are more effective. It all comes from recognizing the patterns and making the alterations.

What the Words Have in Common

Each word at the beginning of the chapter is in reverse alphabetical order.

Comparing Selected NFHS Rule and USSF/FIFA Law Differences

As of February 1, 2000
Dan C. Heldman
(USSF National Instructor Trainer)

Topic	NFHS	USSF/FIFA
Length of Half	40 minutes (Varsity)	Regular: 45 minutes Youth: Varied, based on age
Length of Halftime	10 minutes	Up to 15 minutes
Substitutions: When	GK, Own TI, Own CK, Goal, Half, Injury, Caution or Ejection	Regular: Any stoppage Youth: Own TI, GK, Goal, Injury, Half
Substitutions: Number	Unlimited	Regular: Up to 3 Youth: Unlimited
Substitutions: Procedure	Report to scorer or official **prior** to stoppage for GK, TI, CK restart (otherwise cannot enter the field)	No similar requirement
Substitutions: Injury and Play Stopped	Can treat on field, player must leave, may be substituted	Cannot be treated on field (unless life-threatening or dangerous), Need not be substituted
Substitutions: Return	Substituted player can return to the field	Regular: Cannot return to the field Youth: Can return to the field
Substitutions: Caution	Cautioned player MUST leave until next substitution opportunity (may be substituted)	No similar requirement
Team Roster	Submitted five minutes prior to match: includes players, substitutes, bench personnel	Submitted prior to start of play: includes players and substituted
Equipment: Casts	Illegal, unless covered by padding AND accompanied by release signed by MD	Illegal if considered by referee to be dangerous
Equipment: Uniforms	Home: white or light Visitor: dark	No similar requirement

Topic	NFHS	USSF/FIFA
Equipment: Jewelry	Not permitted (medical bracelets or medals must be taped and showing the medical data)	Not permitted unless clearly religious or medical in nature and not dangerous
Equipment: Braces	Illegal, unless hinges covered and hard surfaces padded	Illegal if considered dangerous by referee
Systems of Control	Dual, Single, 3 whistle, DSC	Single or DSC
Timing	Stadium clock controlled by timekeeper (otherwise kept by referee). Stops for PK, caution, ejection, injury, or as ordered by referee. Restarts when ball is in play again.	Referee keeps time, takes into account time lost but amount is discretionary
Keeper: Illegally changed with field player	Both replacement keeper and prior keeper WARNED at next stoppage of play	Both replacement keeper and prior keeper CAUTIONED at next stoppage of play
Restart: After stoppage OTHER than for foul or misconduct	IFK if one team has clear possession; otherwise DB (Location: where ball was, except in GA)	DB under all circumstances (Location: where ball was, except in GA)
Restart: After stoppage for misconduct off the field or by nonplayer	IFK for team not involved in misconduct (Location: where ball was, except in GA)	DB under all circumstances (Location: where ball was, except in GA)
Dropped Ball	One player from each team (no one else may participate or interfere)	No similar requirement
Ejected Player	May be replaced if ejection occurs during half, quarter, or overtime breaks between periods of play	No replacement under any circumstances
Dangerous Play Violation	Any act considered by referee likely to cause injury to any player (including self) but requires another player to be within playing distance	Any act considered by referee to be dangerous AND which causes opponent to lose opportunity for challenge (requires opponent within playing distance)
Second Caution: Consequence	Player with second caution CAN be replaced	Player with second caution CANNOT be replaced

Topic	NFHS	USSF/FIFA
Second Caution: Mechanics	Yellow/red cards displayed together in same hand	Yellow card displayed, put away, and red card displayed
Cautions and Ejections	Referee required to notify coach, scorer, and officials as to reason	No similar requirement
Signals	Use official NFHS signals (including offside and timeout)	Use USSF/FIFA signals (no signal for offside or timeout)
Foul: by defense to prevent goal	Send off whether successful or not	Send off only if unsuccessful
Misconduct: By other than players or substitutes	Coaches, trainers, or other bench personnel (on roster) may be cautioned or ejected and shown the yellow or red card	No one other than a player or substitute on roster can be cautioned or sent off (or shown a yellow or red card). Such persons can be required to leave the field under threat of game termination.
Foul: "Trickery" in "Pass Back" to Keeper	No caution for player, keeper is penalized only on handling	Keeper need not handle, player committing trickery is cautioned
Foul: Charging the Keeper	Not permitted within PA unless keeper is obstructing and is dribbling the ball	No similar requirement
Misconduct: Incidental vulgar or profane language	Caution	No similar requirement (may be USB at referee's discretion)
Misconduct: Taunting	Send off, with replacement	No similar requirement (may be USB at referee's discretion)
Captains	Team Representative, may request interpretation or essential information	No similar requirement
Restart: Play stopped SOLELY for misconduct by player on the field	IFK where ball was when play was stopped (except in GA)	IFK where misconduct occurred (except in GA)
Substitution: Penalty Kick	Only for injury, caution, or ejection and substitute cannot take PK	No similar requirement

Topic	NFHS	USSF/FIFA
Termination	Host institution up to opening whistle, referee thereafter	Referee determination
Substitutions: Wasting time	Referee orders time clock stopped during substitutions and notifies coach of offending team (potential USC)	No similar requirement (referee discretion)
Coin toss	Winner decides goal to defend or kicking first	Winner decides goal to defend, other team kicks first
Outcome of terminated game	Referee declares game official if one complete half or more has been played	No similar requirement
Second whistle	Required to restart play for PK, after substitution, after caution, ejection, injury, or encroachment	Signal (not necessarily by whistle) required only for PK and KO or where referee is controlling the restart
Drop Ball	Required restart if ball is caused to leave the field by two opponents simultaneously or for simultaneous fouls of same degree by opponents	No similar requirement, referees are advised to decide for one team or another ("simultaneous fouls" are assumed not to occur)
Foul: Kick or attempt to kick the ball while in the keeper's possession	IFK	DFK
Penalty Kick: Violation by kicker	Retake PK	Allow PK to occur, retake only if goal is scored
Penalty Kick: Violation by attacking team	IFK if ball rebounds into play from Keeper or goal structure	IFK only if ball rebounds to infringing attacker
Throw-in	Ball is delivered using equal force by both hands	No similar requirement
Misconduct: Encroachments	If play is allowed to continue (e.g., encroachment by attacker and ball is saved by Keeper), caution for infringement at next stoppage	Infringements of Law 14 are not cautioned except on repetition
Fewer than seven players	Referee can suspend play if a player is off the field temporarily (e.g., equipment)	Referee can allow play to continue if the fewer than seven condition is temporary

Topic	NFHS	USSF/FIFA
Roster: Adding players	May be added after roster is given to referee	May NOT be added after roster is given to referee
Injury: Unconscious	Player rendered unconscious during play cannot return without written authorization by physician	No similar requirement
Injury: Coaching	Coaching instruction to any player is not permitted during time when a coach or trainer is on field attending an injured player	No similar requirement
Injury: Exit from field	An injured player must leave the field if play has been stopped and a coach, trainer, or attendant has been waved onto the field	No similar requirement
Foul: Contact with the ball following reflexive movement to protect self	DFK for handling, if hand or arms move after ball is in motion	USSF advises against considering this an offense if the referee judges the action to be reflexive and no advantage is taken after contact occurs

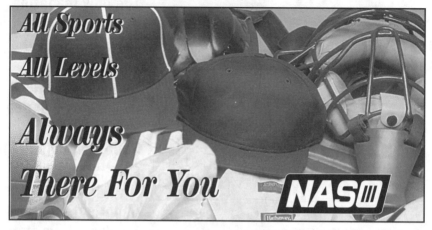

The National Association of Sports Officials

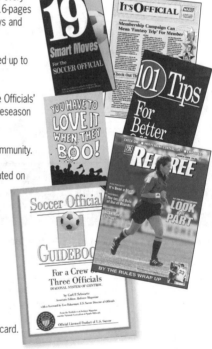

- NASO's "Members Only Edition" of *Referee* magazine every month. Members receive 96-pages of *Referee* with 16-pages of association news, "members only" tips, case plays and ducational product discounts.

- Members receive a *FREE* educational publication valued up to $9.95.

- Discounts on NASO/*Referee* publications such as the Officials' Guidebooks, rules comparisons and sport-specific preseason publications make you a better official.

- Referral service in the event you move to another community.

- Web page and e-mail communications keep you updated on NASO news, services and benefits.

- "Ask Us" rules interpretations service.

- Sports-specific rules quizzes.

- Free NASO e-mail address.

- Free access to the *NASO LockerRoom* — an NASO cyberspace service.

- Membership Certificate and laminated membership card.

- NASO Code of Ethics.

For a complete brochure and membership information contact:
NASO • 2017 Lathrop Avenue • Racine, WI 53405
262/632-5448 • 262/632-5460 (fax)
naso@naso.org or visit our website at www.naso.org